Twelve St

Dick B.'s Reference Titles on Alcoholics Anonymous History

Paradise Research Publications, Inc., Publisher;

Good Book Publishing Company, Distributor P.O. Box 837, Kihei, HI 96753-0837

Phone/Fax: (808) 874 4876; Email: dickb@dickb.com; URL: http://www.dickb.com/index.shtml

Publisher's December 1, 2005 List of Titles by Author Dick B.; All list prices: Effective December 1, 2005

Anne Smith's Journal, 1933-1939, 3rd ed.; 1998; 6 x 9; 180 pp.; $16.95

By the Power of God: A Guide to Early A.A. Groups & Forming Similar Groups Today; 2000, 6 x 9; 260 pp., $16.95

Cured!: Proven Help for Alcoholics and Addicts; 2003, 6 x 9; 182 pp., $17.95

Dr. Bob and His Library, 3rd ed.; 1998; 6 x 9; 156 pp.; $15.95

God and Alcoholism: Our Growing Opportunity in the 21st Century; 2002; 6 x 9; 190 pp.; $17.95

Good Morning!: Quiet Time, Morning Watch, Meditation, and Early A.A.; 2d ed.; 1998; 6 x 9; 154 pp.; $16.95

Henrietta B. Seiberling: Ohio's Lady with a Cause, Rev. ed.; 2004; 46 pp.; 8 ½ x 11; spiral bound, $15.95

Making Known The Biblical History and Roots of Alcoholics Anonymous: An Eleven-Year Research, Writing, Publishing and Fact Dissemination Project, 2001, 160 pp., spiral bound, $24.95

New Light on Alcoholism: God, Sam Shoemaker, and A.A.; 2d ed.; 1999; 6 x 9; 672 pp.; $24.95

The Akron Genesis of Alcoholics Anonymous, 2d ed.; 1998; 6 x 9; 400 pp.; $17.95

The Books Early AAs Read for Spiritual Growth, 7th ed.; 1998; 6 x 9; 126 pp.; $15.95

The First Nationwide A.A. History Conference - Comments of Dick B., 2003, 8 ½ x 11, 79 pp., spiral bound, $17.95

The Golden Text of A.A.: God, the Pioneers, and Real Spirituality; 1999; 6 x 9; 76 pp.; $14.95

The Good Book and The Big Book: A.A.'s Roots in the Bible; 2d ed.; 1997; 6 x 9; 264 pp.; $17.95

The James Club: The Original A.A. Program's Absolute Essentials, 3rd ed., 2005; 6 x 9; $17.95

The Oxford Group & Alcoholics Anonymous, 2d ed.; 1998; 6 x 9; 432 pp.; $17.95

That Amazing Grace (Clarence & Grace S.); 1996; 6 x 9; 160 pp.; $16.95

Turning Point: A History of Early A.A.'s Spiritual Roots and Successes; 1997; 6 x 9; 776 pp.; $29.95

Twelve Steps for You: Let Our Creator, A.A. History, and the Big Book Be Your Guide; 2003; 6 x 9; 90 pp. $17.95

Utilizing Early A.A.'s Spiritual Roots for Recovery Today; Rev. ed.; 1999; 6 x 9; 106 pp., $14.95

When Early AA s Were Cured and Why; 2003; 8 ½ x 11; spiral bound; 114 pp.; $17.95

Why Early A.A. Succeeded: The Good Book in Alcoholics Anonymous Yesterday and Today (a Bible Study Primer), 2001; 6 x 9; 340 pp., $17.95

Available through other distributors

Hope: The Story of Geraldine O. Delaney, 2d ed. NJ: Alina Lodge

Our Faith Community A.A. Legacy (Dick B., ed and compiler). FL: Came to Believe Publications

Courage to Change (with Bill Pittman). MN: Hazelden

Women Pioneers of AA (Dick B., contributor). MN: Hazelden

Twelve Steps for You

Take the Twelve Steps with the Big Book, A.A. History, and the Good Book at Your Side

Dick B.

Historian, Bible Student, Retired Attorney, Recovered AA
(Author of 26 Titles on Early A.A.'s Spiritual Roots)

Paradise Research Publications, Inc.
Kihei, Maui, Hawaii

Paradise Research Publications, Inc.
PO Box 837
Kihei, HI 96753-0837
(808 874 4876)
Email: dickb@dickb.com
URL: http://www.dickb.com/index.shtml

This Paradise Research Publications Edition is published by arrangement with Good Book Publishing Company, PO Box 837, Kihei, HI: 96753-0837

The publication of this volume does not imply affiliation with, nor approval or endorsement from Alcoholics Anonymous World Services, Inc. The views expressed herein are solely those of the author. A.A. is a program of recovery from alcoholism–use of the Twelve Steps in connection with programs and activities which are patterned after A.A. but which address other problems, does not imply otherwise.

Note: All Bible verses quoted in this book, unless otherwise noted, are from the Authorized (or "King James") Version. The letters "KJV" are used when necessary to distinguish it from other versions.

ISBN 1-885803-98-2

Contents

Introduction

The Actual Origins of the Twelve Steps

They did not come from A.A. co-founder Dr. Bob, who said quite plainly:

> I didn't write the Twelve Steps. I had nothing to do with the writing of them. We already had the basic ideas, though not in terse and tangible form. We got them . . . as a result of our study of the Good Book (*DR. BOB and the Good Oldtimers*. NY: Alcoholics Anonymous World Services, Inc., 1980, p. 96).

They did not originate with A.A. co-founder Bill W. who–though he wrote them–clearly pointed elsewhere when he discussed their sources:

> . . . Frank Amos, a newspaper and advertising executive and a Trustee of A.A., only lately retired, [in] 1938 went out to Akron to meet Dr. Bob and to make a careful survey of what had transpired there. It was his glowing report of Dr. Bob and Akron's Group Number One that had caught Mr. Rockefeller's interest and had further encouraged the formation of the [Alcoholic] Foundation (*Twelve Steps and Twelve Traditions*. NY: Alcoholics Anonymous Publishing, Inc., 1952, pp. 15-16).

> The basic principles of A.A., as they are known today, were borrowed mainly from the fields of religion and medicine, though some ideas upon which success finally depended were the result of noting the behavior and needs of the fellowship itself (*Twelve Steps and Twelve Traditions*, *supra*, p.16).

> The basic principles which the Oxford Groupers had taught were ancient and universal ones, the common property of mankind. . . . the early A.A. got its ideas of self-examination, acknowledgment of character defects, restitution for harm done, and working with others straight from the Oxford Groups and directly from Sam Shoemaker, their former leader in America,

and from nowhere else *(Twelve Steps and Twelve Traditions, supra*, p. 39).

So far as I am concerned, and Dr. Smith too, the O.G. [Oxford Group] seeded A.A. It was our spiritual wellspring at the beginning (Letter from William G. Wilson to Samuel M. Shoemaker, 14 July 1949, a copy of which Dick B. inspected at the archives at Bill W.'s Stepping Stones home at Bedford Hills, New York).

I am always glad to say privately that some of the Oxford Group presentation and emphasis upon the Christian message saved my life (Quoting Bill Wilson. See *Pass It On.* NY: Alcoholics Anonymous World Services, Inc., 1984, p. 171).

As a society we must never become so vain as to suppose that we are authors and inventors of a new religion. We will humbly reflect that every one of A.A.'s principles has been borrowed from ancient sources (*As Bill Sees It.* NY: Alcoholics Anonymous World Services, Inc., 1967, p. 223).

Bill Wilson found himself in awe of Dr. Bob's "spiritual knowledge" and cherished the guidance of Anne Smith as each morning her pleasant voice read and interpreted the Christian Scriptures and the Oxford Group devotional books (Ernest Kurtz, *Not-God: A History of Alcoholics Anonymous,* exp ed. MN: Hazelden, 1991, p. 32).

A.A. was not invented! Its basics were brought to us through the experience and wisdom of many great friends. We simply borrowed and adapted their ideas (*As Bill Sees It. supra*, p. 67).

Nor were they simply borrowed from discussions by Dr. Bob and Bill W., but rather, from the Bible, the Oxford Group, Sam Shoemaker, and some other successful Akron practices:

This was the beginning of A.A.'s 'flying blind period.' They had the Bible, and they had the precepts of the Oxford Group. . . . They were working, or working out, the A.A. program–the Twelve Steps–without quite knowing how they were doing it (*DR. BOB and the Good Oldtimers*, *supra*, p. 96).

I learned a great deal from you people [T. Henry and Clarace Williams], from the Smiths themselves, and from Henrietta

[Seiberling]. I hadn't looked in the Bible, up to this time, at all. You see, I had the . . . [conversion] experience first and then this rushing around to help drunks and nothing happened (Taped remarks of Bill Wilson in December 12, 1954. See Dick B., *The Akron Genesis of Alcoholics Anonymous*, 2d ed. Kihei, HI: Paradise Research Publications, Inc., 1998, p. 10).

The four absolutes [of the Oxford Group], as we called them, were the only yardsticks we had in the early days, before the Steps. I think the absolutes still hold good and can be extremely helpful (Quoting Dr. Bob in *The Co-Founders of Alcoholics Anonymous* (NY: Alcoholics Anonymous World Headquarters, 1972, 1975, pp. 12-13).

Of course the Bible ought to be the main Source Book of all. No day ought to pass without reading it (Quote from journal kept by Dr. Bob's wife. See Dick B., *Anne Smith's Journal, 1933-1939.* 3rd ed. Kihei, HI: Paradise Research Publications, Inc., 1998, pp. 12-13).

They [the early AAs] were convinced that the answer to their problems was in the Good Book. To some of us older ones, the parts we found absolutely essential were the Sermon on the Mount, the 13th chapter of First Corinthians, and the Book of James (Quoting Dr. Bob, from *DR. BOB and the Good Oldtimers, supra*, p. 96).

Quite clearly, therefore, you will find the origins of the Twelve Steps in the Bible; the principles of the Oxford Group; and the actual language of Rev. Sam Shoemaker, Rector of Calvary Episcopal Church in New York, together with items borrowed from Anne Smith, Dr. Bob's wife, Dr. Carl Jung, Professor William James, Dr. William Silkworth, Richard Peabody, and the practical experience working with alcoholics in Akron and New York.

From the Roots to the Fruits

Factoring into Your Understanding the Events from Dr. Bob's Youth to June, 1935

Dr. Bob acquired his Biblical ideas in, and applied them in his religious practices from, his days as a youngster in St. Johnsbury, Vermont, through his days as an Akron physician in 1935

From childhood through high school, I was more or less forced to go to church, Sunday school and evening service, Monday night Christian Endeavor, and sometimes to Wednesday-evening prayer meeting (Quoting Dr. Bob from *DR. BOB*, *supra*, p. 12).

We [Bill Wilson and Dr. Bob] had both been associated with the Oxford Group, Bill in New York, for five months, and I in Akron, for two and a half years. Bill had acquired their idea of service. I had not, but I had done an immense amount of reading they had recommended. I had refreshed my memory of the Good Book, and I had had excellent training in that as a youngster (Quoting Dr. Bob from *The Co-Founders*, *supra*, p. 7).

Before there was a Big Book–in the period of "flying blind," God's Big Book was the reference used in our home. The summer of 1935, when Bill lived with us, Dr. Bob had read the Bible completely three times. And the references that seemed consistent with the program goals were the Sermon on the Mount, 1 Corinthians 13, and the Book of James (Quoting Dr. Bob's son in his Foreword in Dick B., *The Good Book and The Big Book: A.A.'s Roots in the Bible.* 2d ed. Kihei, HI: Paradise Research Publications, Inc., 1998, p. ix).

Bill W. acquired his Oxford Group ideas beginning in 1934 and then from that date through the end of 1938 directly from the Group's American leader Sam Shoemaker

Bill's friend Ebby Thacher had learned and passed along to Bill specifics about the Oxford Group from three friends–former drunkards–Shep Cornell, Cebra Graves, and Rowland Hazard (*Pass It On.* NY: Alcoholics Anonymous World Services, Inc., 1984, pp. 113-114).

During several visits to Bill Wilson at Towns Hospital in New York, Ebby Thacher told Bill Wilson of his former hopeless drinking condition, of his getting religion, of what God had done for him that he couldn't do for himself, and the specifics of his Oxford Group learning (*Pass It On*, *supra*, pp. 116-117).

And, in the next few years, Wilson himself got the spiritual substance of all of the Steps, particularly the last ten Steps, straight from his own earlier association with the Oxford Groups as they were then led in America by the Episcopal rector, Dr. Samuel M. Shoemaker (*The Language of the Heart*. NY: The AA Grapevine, Inc., 1988, pp. 202, 298, 177).

There are also demonstrable additional sources of Bill's Big Book and Twelve Step ideas

These certainly included the opinion of, and advice to, Rowland Hazard by Dr. Carl Jung that there was no cure for the mind of the chronic alcoholic without a religious "conversion" (*Pass It On*, *supra*, pp. 114, 381-386).

They included the opinion of, and advice to Bill W. by, Dr. William Duncan Silkworth, Bill's psychiatrist at Towns Hospital, that Bill would have little success helping other alcoholics without telling them about the illness of alcoholism that condemned them to go mad or die if they continued to drink (*Pass It On.*, *supra*, p. 133).

They included the opinion of, and book by, Professor William James of Harvard (deceased by the time Bill had read him) that the kind of religious experience Wilson believed he had encountered in Towns Hospital was a valid one and constituted a necessary turning point in any religious life–and which was a conversion experience resulting from a crisis of self-surrender (*Pass It On*, *supra*, pp. 120-125).

Unquestionably too, as we now can see, they included some lay therapy ideas and phrases which Wilson also borrowed. These theories had to do with the supposed inability to cure alcoholism, the inadequacy of "half measures," and the importance of relaxation techniques and "suggestion" (See Richard R. Peabody. *The Common Sense of Drinking*. Atlantic Monthly Press Book, 1939; Dick B., *Comments at The First Nationwide Alcoholics Anonymous History Conference*. Kihei, HI: Paradise Research Publications, Inc., 2003).

Finally, they included lingo from "New Thought" and metaphysical writers such as Emmet Fox, Mary Baker Eddy,

William James, Emanuel Swedenborg, Ralph Waldo Trine, and Thomas Troward. From these sources, albeit intermingled, came such Wilson Big Book phrases as "Creative Intelligence" (*Alcoholics Anonymous*, 4th ed., pp. 12, 46, 49), "Spirit of Nature" (p. 12), "Spirit of the Universe" (pp. 10, 46, 52, 75), "Great Reality" (p. 161), "Infinite Power" (p. 56), "world of the Spirit" (p. 84), "Higher Power" (pp. 43, 101) "Universal Mind" (p. 12), "fourth dimension of existence" (p. 8), and similar transcendent verbiage (For bibliography on the contributing writings, see Dick B., *The Books Early AAs Read for Spiritual Growth*, 7th ed., Kihei, HI: Paradise Research Publications, Inc.).

The first concrete A.A. program was developed between 1935 and 1938, and was reported and detailed by Frank Amos to his principal, John D. Rockefeller, Jr. in 1938

At the behest of John D. Rockefeller, Jr., Frank Amos came to Akron in 1938 and then rendered two reports on the essence of the Christian technique achieving so much success with Dr. Bob as the fellowship's leader; and we will cover this shortly.

The significance of Wilson's varied and divergent summaries of six 'word-of-mouth' ideas

We will also discuss several varied and conflicting ways in which Bill Wilson chose to describe "an" earlier "word-of-mouth" program which consisted of six steps and which he used to expand into, and to fashion, his own Twelve Steps in the Big Book.

The intended importance of the basic text's personal stories before Wilson expanded his manuscript and completed in full the actual First Edition of Alcoholics Anonymous.

The drafts of the proposed Big Book—drafts and an outline—which I discovered at the Wilson home (called "Stepping Stones") at Bedford Hills, New York, make clear that the text book was originally intended to parallel the Oxford Group life-changing technique of "sharing for witness"–of telling stories about what God had done for the afflicted that they could not do for themselves. And much effort was expended by the Akron crew, led by Dr. Bob, pulling together a variety of success stories that wound up almost exclusively in the back of the First

Edition of the Big Book. Actually, in these stories–found in the First Edition of *Alcoholics Anonymous* published in 1939–you see real traces of the early Akron program from the frequent mention of the Bible, prayer, and Bible passages (1st ed, pp. 205, 215, 227, 263-264, 322-323, 335, 347, 359, 363, 377, God (pp. 214-216, 218, 221, 224, 236-237, 240-241, 249, 270-271-273, 285-286, etc.) the Almighty (pp. 213, 359, Jesus Christ (pp. 295, 379), and so on.

Bill's pulling the actual Twelve Steps together primarily from Shoemaker

As you study the correspondence between Bill Wilson and Sam Shoemaker, the conferences they had, and the request by Bill that Sam write the Twelve Steps, you find yourself looking for, and quickly seeing, Shoemaker language—words and phrases that pertain to the "step" ideas—that appear on many pages of the Big Book text. (See Dick B., *New Light on Alcoholism: God, Sam Shoemaker, and A.A.*, 2d ed. Kihei, HI: Paradise Research Publications, Inc., 1999).

Fashioning the "God compromise"and adding the "universalizing" New Thought language

Examine the first draft of the Twelve Steps (as reconstructed by A.A. writers). Consider the alterations and deletions made in their language pertaining to God. Note the tossing out of some 400 pages allegedly Christian in their content. And take into account the assertion by Lois Wilson that there had been a supposed "agreement" to universalize the Big Book and eliminate Christian connotations (*Pass It On*, *supra*, pp. 196-204; *Lois Remembers*. NY: Al-Anon Family Group Headquarters, Inc., 1987, pp. 113-115, 109). If you take the time to do this, you will then realize that the text of Bill's 1939 Big Book is not at all representative of the Christian program utilized by Akron AAs between 1935 and 1939 - and even thereafter.

The Steps and Stories As Originally Proposed, and the Alterations

The Twelve Steps as originally written can truly be said to be the work of Bill Wilson's hand, and his alone. I have searched high and low for the original manuscript and never been able to locate it. But A.A. itself asserts that the following is an accurate replica, reconstructed by the A.A. authors of *Pass It On*. See **the reconstruction of the Original Twelve Steps as set forth in *Pass It On, supra*, pp. 198-99:**

1. We admitted we were powerless over alcohol—that our lives had become unmanageable.
2. Came to believe that God could restore us to sanity.
3. Made a decision to turn our wills and our lives over to the care and direction of God.
4. Made a searching and fearless moral inventory of ourselves.
5. Admitted to God, to ourselves, and to another human being the exact nature of our wrongs.
6. Were entirely willing that God remove all these defects of character.
7. Humbly on our knees asked Him to remove these shortcomings—holding nothing back.
8. Made a complete list of all persons we had harmed, and became willing to make amends to them all.
9. Made direct amends to such people wherever possible, except when to do so would injure them or others.
10. Continued to take personal inventory and when we were wrong promptly admitted it.
11. Sought through prayer and meditation to improve our contact with God, praying only for knowledge of His will for us and the power to carry that out.
12. Having had a spiritual experience as the result of this course of action, we tried to carry this message to others, especially alcoholics, and to practice these principles in all our affairs.

The presently missing manuscript pages that were tossed out prior to publication of the First Edition of the Big Book.

Pass It On, supra, states at page 204:

Final Editing of the book was done by Tom Uzzell, member of the faculty at New York University. Uzzell cut the book by at least a third (some say half–from 800 to 400 pages).

To locate and verify the contents of these missing pages, I endeavored mightily but without success to locate Uzzell in New York and elsewhere. I visited the archives at N.Y.U and was told there were no Uzzell papers there. I contacted my friends Nell Wing and Frank Mauser, A.A.'s first and second archivists, respectively. Neither could shed light on the destroyed materials. I contacted the heir of the papers owned by a private secretary to both Bill Wilson and Lois Wilson. He believed he had seen the full, prior manuscript, but could not find it after an extensive search by both of us of his home and papers. I contacted the two successive principal authors of *Pass It On*. Not one of the foregoing people was able to recall, locate, or verify the content of the deleted material. But the last actual writer of *Pass It On* (the person who completed the title as published) assured me that, although she could not remember the source of the quote about Uzzell's editing, she knew that the *Pass It On* statement had verifiable roots and was accurate.

Bill Pittman, presently Director of Historical Information at Hazelden, personally informed me that Ruth Hock (the woman who had been Wilson's secretary and typed the Big Book manuscript pages) told him (Pittman) that the missing materials that were tossed out consisted primarily of those containing Christian language and ideas. Ruth's recollection appears to be consistent with the account of the battle among Wilson, Hank Parkhurst, and John Henry Fitzhugh Mayo over keeping Christian materials in the Big Book. "Fitz" was the son of an Episcopal minister. He became a close friend of Bill and Lois Wilson and was one of the few, early New York success stories. And when objections arose over the word "God" in the proposed Big Book, Fitz argued insistently that the Big Book should go "all the way with God." Fitz also "insisted (albeit unsuccessfully) that the book should express Christian doctrines and use Biblical terms and expressions" (See *Pass It On*, pp. 198-199, 161-169). It is therefore rather clear to me that we will never know just what the Big Book contained of a specific Biblical or Christian nature before the final draft. And, when my son and I spent a week researching at the Episcopal Church Archives in Austin, Texas, we carefully examined 58 boxes of the papers of Rev. Sam Shoemaker, Jr., and found that most of the Shoemaker-Wilson correspondence covering the critical drafting period from 1935 to 1939, has simply vanished. It was apparently lifted from the archives, removed, and taken elsewhere without authorization. There is correspondence referring to the material, but it was never returned to its rightful owner—the Episcopal Church Archives. We did see there written correspondence from Sam Shoemaker to Bill Wilson in which Shoemaker told Wilson he had been in "closest" touch with Wilson from 1934 to the publication date in 1939. Shoemaker said he had been provided with a copy of the "manuscript." Yet the manuscript's absence from A.A. General Services, from Stepping Stones, and from the Shoemaker papers at the Episcopal Church Archives, coupled with the inability of all the principals to recall the actual facts contained in the missing manuscript, seem to put them this vital historical fragment beyond history's reach. We do know for a certainty, however, that the Christian Fellowship program of Akron passed from existence with the final manuscript for the Big Book.

The five vital "musts" of the original Akron program that were not a part of the Steps as finally drafted:

We summarize here the five major parts of the seven part Akron "program" as Frank Amos reported its "vital" parts to Rockefeller in February of 1938 (See *DR. BOB*, *supra*, pp. 130-131):

1. An alcoholic must realize that he is an alcoholic, incurable from a medical standpoint, and that he must never again drink anything with alcohol in it.

2. He must surrender himself absolutely to God, realizing that in himself there is no hope.

3. He must remove from his life other sins such as hatred, adultery, and others which frequently accompany alcoholism.

4. He must have devotions every morning—a "quiet time" of prayer and some reading from the Bible and other religious literature.

5. He must be willing to help other alcoholics get straightened out.

But some remnants of the Akron program did survive the elimination of Bible, prayer, and Jesus Christ from the First Edition personal stories:

If you examine the foregoing points of the Akron program, you will be hard-pressed to see any comparable similarities that survived in the basic text of the Big Book. "Incurable from a medical standpoint" was changed to "incurable." Though AAs had claimed for the first decade that they were *cured* (See Big Book 4th ed, p. 191 where Bill W. and Bill D. both stated they were cured), Wilson deleted mention of this, and stated in one sentence that there is no "cure" for alcoholism. "God" (Yahweh, the Creator, the Maker, Spirit) was altered and converted into some nebulous "higher power." The reference to "sins" was removed. "Quiet Time," "Bible," and "religious literature" were altered and removed. And "principles"--a vague expression lacking definition--were mentioned but not defined in the Twelfth Step, whereas the Pioneers spoke of the Four Absolutes, the Beatitudes, 1 Corinthians 13, the Ten Commandments, and other Bible teachings that very clearly laid out the principles they tried to practice. The same lack does not seem true in the personal stories in the First Edition of the big Book. For one thing, they were written primarily by or for Akron people, and we leave it to the student to decide if the personal accounts should be studied to determine more about the real Akron program.

The Predominance of Oxford Group/Shoemaker ideas in the final Basic Text

As almost fifteen years of research have made evident to me, and as the authors of *Pass It On* also observed, the basic text of A.A.'s Big Book is Oxford Group and Shoemaker in content and path–the path being the path it suggested as a way to finding, and establishing a relationship with God. There remain a smattering of Bible verses quoted without attribution; and there remains the strong (but seldom admitted) influence of the Bible on almost every idea which Wilson, Smith, the Oxford Group, Sam Shoemaker, and the religious authors utilized in their remarks and writings.

The Importance to You of Knowing All the Sources

What happens when you don't know them:

Without access to the roots of A.A., you are subjected in meetings and recovery writings, A.A. and otherwise, to self-made nonsense gods, manufactured "spirituality," misinterpreted Biblical "guidance," misunderstood Biblical principles taken out of context, and the presence of added practices that were never a part of the original Akron success program.

What the Big Book and Steps say to you when you do have the benefit of, learn, and know their sources:

It is then no longer difficult to see that A.A.'s basic ideas *did* come from the Good Book—just as Dr. Bob said they did. You almost immediately recognize that the life-changing ideas of the Oxford Group and

Shoemaker are still very much in evidence in the AA program. Those Oxford Group principles were the principles of the Bible. You discern that Yahweh, the Creator—not some sanitized, universalized nonsense god that is called a radiator, a door knob, or a tree—was the subject of the program, whatever Lois Wilson may have thought or her husband may have arranged in Ruth Hock's office to toss out. Moreover, you relate easily to Dr. Bob's statement that the absolutely essential principles were primarily taken from the Book of James, the Sermon on the Mount, and 1 Corinthians 13–just as Dr. Bob said they were. You also recognize that the "code" of "love and tolerance" and the major purpose of service to God and your fellow man (as declared in the Big Book) can be found planted in the two great commandments of Jesus–to love God and love your neighbor. Also, you are no longer awash in the confused talk at meetings which ignores the Bible, as well as possible revelation from God, as the means for learning and knowing Almighty God and His will. You can also then rest assured that, whatever road the present fellowship, its leaders, and its individual members, may choose to pursue, A.A.'s original path to the oft-mentioned relationship with God–access to God–as the Big Book puts it, was through Jesus Christ as the way, the truth, and the life (See John 14:6: "Jesus saith unto him, I am the way, the truth, and the life: no man cometh unto the Father, but by me"). And this rock provides ample explanation as to why the early Akron AAs all were required in their Christian Fellowship to surrender on their knees and accept Jesus Christ as their Lord and Saviour.

A.A.'s major sources and their specifics that can be learned from the Dick B. titles:

The six major sources of the Big Book and its Twelve Steps were the Bible, Quiet Time, Anne Smith, the Oxford Group, Shoemaker, and the Christian literature read by the Pioneers.

The basic Biblical ideas were later either displaced or mixed up with non-biblical ideas: allergy, obsession, religious experience, spiritual awakening, nonsense gods, lack of a power to cure, and private interpretation of God's will.

I finally realized that there is an additional major source, The United Christian Endeavor Society, which seems, by reason of Dr. Bob's active membership in it in his youth, to have passed along to Dr. Bob and, in turn, to A.A. itself the major features of the Akron program—Christian Fellowship, acceptance of Christ, Bible study, group prayer meetings, conversions, Quiet Hour, reading of Christian literature, support for one's church, love, and service. These features were part and parcel of the Akron program and really had nothing to do with the Oxford Group or Sam Shoemaker. This seventh major source is still being researched by me and by others. See http://www.dickb.com/Christian_Endeavor.shtml for a timely research article. I have recently written and incorporated into latest new title, *The James Club*, a specific review of the Christian Endeavor influence on Akron A.A.—not particularly Bill's Oxford Group-oriented Big Book and Twelve Steps.

The doors open to all AAs of every religion and creed, once they do know the sources

The Bible, and not G.S.O publication's personal views, becomes your standard for truth on spiritual matters.

The way to Christian faith still remains open to, and a choice for, those who currently are confused by the bizarre language in present-day meetings, and are often openly rebuked for making religious and Christian remarks that were commonplace in pioneer A.A.

A.A.'s all too apparent, current "universalism" can be treated as a fact instead of a faith.

The Oxford Group becomes a tool for understanding instead of a supposedly discarded root that is frequently criticized and rejected by some present-day A.A. members who are atheists, secularists, Roman Catholics, Jews, and even Protestants. But A.A. itself loses when members and writers make and fire at targets like the Washingtonians and the Oxford Group. It needs information and understanding, not religious or irreligious prejudice.

The "principles" in the Big Book—even if some are not Biblical in origin or correctness--can still be used as helpful "moral" standards for those who choose to reject what religion and the clergy offered to early A.A., and continue to offer today.

Nonetheless, the opportunity then still exists for a return to, and application of, the early ideas by those who favor A.A., don't want to leave it, want to remain in it or in other life-changing Twelve Step fellowships, and desire to square their A.A. practices with their personal religious convictions.

A.A. can still claim and espouse, within its ranks, non-sectarian, non-denominational, non-controversial integrity—but these alleged virtues ring hollow every time some secularist bashes away at the Bible, the churches, religion, God, and Jesus Christ in meetings and A.A. literature. Our guide—this guide--can simplify, and assist in the use and study of, the Bible, the Big Book, and Twelve Steps; and it can and should be supplemented with my own historical reference titles that fully and accurately explain the substance and details of the early A.A. program.

Part 1:

Begin your step study by reviewing the Original Akron Program and learning how A.A. really began

There are many helpful descriptions by those who founded, investigated, and supported early Akron A.A.

Albert Scott, a Rockefeller representative, and chairman of the trustees for Riverside Church, said of the original Akron program:

> Why, this is first-century Christianity! What can we do to help? (*Pass It On*, *supra*, p. 184).

Frank Amos, who investigated it for Rockefeller, and later became an A.A. trustee, said:

> . . . in many respects, their meetings have taken on the form of the meetings described in the Gospels [*sic*] of the early Christians during the first century (*DR. BOB*, *supra*, pp. 135-136).

Bill Wilson told of the reading from the Bible each morning by Dr. Bob's wife Anne, and said:

> James was our favorite. Reading from her chair in the corner, she would softly conclude, "Faith without works is dead." This was a favorite quotation of Anne's, much as the Book of James was a favorite with early A.A.'s–so much so that "The James Club" was favored by some as a name for the Fellowship (*DR. BOB*, *supra*, p. 71).

Dr. Bob called every Akron meeting of the society a "Christian fellowship"

1

(See *DR. BOB*, *supra*, p. 118. See also the validation of this statement by Dr. Bob's daughter to me personally, by pioneer Bob E., and by the Oxford Group itself, Dick B., *The Akron Genesis of Alcoholics Anonymous*, 2d ed. Kihei, HI: Paradise Research Publications, Inc., 1998, pp. 219-220, footnotes 3 and 4).

An early A.A. Pioneer gave this impression of what his A.A. friends were passing on:

Here were these men who visited me and they, like myself, had tried everything else and although it was plain to be seen none of them were perfect, they were living proof that the sincere attempt to follow the cardinal teachings of Jesus Christ was keeping them sober (*Alcoholics Anonymous*, 1st ed, 1939, p. 295).

An Overview of What Akron AAs Developed and Did in Akron's Program

Hospitalization for about seven days: Only a Bible in the room, medications, daily visits and lengthy talks with the newcomers by Dr. Bob, visits by recovered pioneers, belief in God, surrender to Christ, and prayer. Then discharge from the hospital.

Recovery work in and from the homes: (1) Daily get-togethers, (2) Bible study and reading—particularly from the Book of James, Jesus' Sermon on the Mount, and 1 Corinthians 13, (3) Individual quiet times, (4) Quiet Times in the morning with Anne Smith, (5) Discussions with Dr. Bob, his wife Anne Smith, and Henrietta Seiberling, (6) A regular Wednesday meeting, with "real" surrenders upstairs (following James 5:15-16 with "Elders" and prayers) involving acceptance of Jesus Christ, asking God to take alcohol out of their lives, and asking Him to help them abide by the Four Absolutes, (7) Observing some additional, individual Oxford Group practices such as Moral Inventory, Confession, Conviction, and Restitution, (8) Visiting newcomers at the hospital, (9) Church attendance by most. (10) Social, religious, and family fellowship.

Regular Wednesday Meetings: Opening prayer, reading of Scripture, group prayer and guidance, Discussion of topics from Bible or devotionals, Surrenders, appeal for helping newcomers, Lord's Prayer, socializing, and exchange of literature. No drunkalogs. No steps. No Big Book. Just Bible and use of devotionals like the *Upper Room.*

Quiet Time (with Anne at the Smith home each morning, with the alcoholic squad and their families, or individually): Based on participants' having accepted Jesus Christ—then engaging in daily Bible reading; prayer and seeking guidance; use of devotionals; use of *Anne Smith's Journal*; and the reading of Christian literature.

Also: If you read the statements Bill and Dr. Bob made together at the Shrine Auditorium in Los Angeles in 1943, here's what you find: There were some 4500 AAs, their families, and their friends present. The reporter this about Bill Wilson actually said:

> "There is a definite religious element here," Bill said. "I pray and I feel released. He   emphasized that Divine Aid was A.A.'s greatest asset, more effective than confinement,   environment changes and dietary experiments" (See Dick B., *Why Early A.A. Succeeded.* Kihei, HI: Paradise Research Publications, Inc., 2001, pp. 6-7, quoting from *The Tidings*,   March 16, 1943, p.17).

The reporter then said this about Dr. Bob's remarks, which were given at the same event on the same stage with Bill Wilson:

> "Read religious literature. Resume church attendance. Cultivate the habit of prayer, and   transmit the desires and principles of Alcoholics Anonymous to others." [He particularly emphasized reading the Bible, said the reporter who covered the talk] (See Dick B., *Why Early A.A. Succeeded, supra*, p. 46, also quoting from *The Tidings*, March 16, 1943, p. 17).

Thus during their joint appearance, Bill spoke about Divine Aid, A.A.'s religious element, and a release through prayer. Dr. Bob spoke about reading religious materials for growth, church attendance for worship and instruction, the need for regular prayer habits, and the importance of reading the Bible. Both men were warmly received; and their unanimity of views was apparent.

The Frank Amos Reports in 1938

Of Akron's "ex-alcoholics" and their program, Rockefeller's investigator Frank Amos said: (1) He had conducted his investigation over a week, and the alcoholic group comprised some 50 men and 2 women. (2) "All [were] considered practically incurable by physicians." (3) They had

3

"been reformed and so far have remained teetotalers." (4) He heard varying stories, "many of them almost miraculous." (5) Despite variances in the stories, "when it came to recovery, they were all remarkably alike in 'the technique used and the system followed'." (6) "Their meetings have taken on the form of the meetings described in the Gospels of the early Christians during the first century" (*DR. BOB*, *supra*, pp. 130-136). Mr. Amos then described their seven-point "Program" as follows:

[Abstinence] An alcoholic must realize that he is an alcoholic, incurable from a medical viewpoint, and that he must never again drink anything with alcohol in it.

[Absolute reliance on the Creator] He must surrender himself absolutely to God, realizing that in himself there is no hope.

[Removal of sins from his life] Not only must he want to stop drinking permanently, he must remove from his life other sins such as hatred, adultery, and others which frequently accompany alcoholism. Unless he will do this absolutely, Smith and his associates refuse to work with him.

[Daily Quiet Time with Bible study and prayer] He must have devotions every morning–a "quiet time" of prayer and some reading from the Bible and other religious literature. Unless this is faithfully followed, there is grave danger of backsliding.

[Helping other alcoholics] He must be willing to help other alcoholics get straightened out. This throws up a protective barrier and strengthens his own willpower and convictions.

[Fellowship] It is important, but not vital, that he meet frequently with other reformed alcoholics and form both a social and a religious comradeship.

[Religious affiliation] Important, but not vital, that he attend some religious service at least once weekly.

For additional details, see Dick B. *God and Alcoholism: Our Growing Opportunity in the 21ˢᵗ Century* (Kihei, HI: Paradise Research Publications, Inc., 2002); and *DR. BOB*, *supra*, p. 131.

Part 2:

Begin Your Study of the Steps by looking first at the Bible and at each Step's Known Bible Origins in Mind

You can find a thorough and detailed elaboration of the basic ideas early AAs took from the Bible in seven of my Dick B. titles: (1) *The Good Book and The Big Book: A.A.'s* Roots *in the Bible.* (2) *Good Morning!: Quiet Time, Morning Watch, Meditation, and Early A.A.* (3) *Why Early A.A. Succeeded: The Good Book in A.A. Yesterday and Today.* (4) *Turning Point: A History of Early A.A.'s Spiritual Roots and Successes.* (5) *By the Power of God: A Guide to Early A.A. Groups and Forming Similar Groups Today.* (6) *When Early AAs Were Cured and Why.* (7) *The James Club*

The importance of accuracy concerning what the A.A. pioneers actually studied in the Bible

Throughout the existence of the A.A. Fellowship, various members, writers, and publishers have listed Bible verses which they felt were **related** to the Twelve Steps. But that is a backward approach if we looking for the truths the pioneers incorporated from the Bible and used to save their very lives. The study of the Bible and the Steps should start first with a look at each step and then an effort to pinpoint the portion of the Bible, if any, that provided the basic step idea. By contrast, most of the presently-listed voluminous and quoted verses were never specifically known to, or related to, anything Dr. Bob, Bill Wilson, Anne Smith, or other pioneers actually mentioned and studied. Later, AAs themselves wrote about Bible ideas in such materials as the *Cleveland Central Bulletin*, the Akron AA pamphlets, and other non-Conference approved literature. Again, the quoted verses were far more the product of individual thinking about the principles, than the fruit of historical investigation. Next came what I call the Twelve Step Bibles where editors and researchers filled almost every page of their Bibles with Twelve Step quotes and comments. Today, a number of fellowships and publishers have begun publishing their own versions of the Twelve Steps–as they believe they *should have been written.* They then packed these revised materials with Bible verses they felt should have been used. The difficulty with all these materials is that they represent someone's ideas about the Bible and recovery, rather than a recitation of the basic ideas early AAs actually studied in, and borrowed from, the Bible. It is one thing to say that most of A.A.'s basic ideas came from the Bible. It is quite another to assign a multitude of Bible verses to some particular Step or concept without first determining what the pioneers really saw in the Bible when they fashioned a step that seem directly related to the Bible. Quoting the Bible out of context often has little or no value. Also, quoting the Bible in context needs also to be accompanied by an evaluation of whether the quoted portion is itself of any value. You can learn the Bible in church, seminary, and Bible fellowship. But, in examining A.A., you need to recognize a Bible source and then determine if it has been corrupted in use to prove a point, rather than express God's view about the point. An effort that quotes the Bible and then tries to find a relationship to the steps is not providing the best service for alcoholics. The latter effort merely indicates a writer's view that the quoted verses are compatible with the quoted A.A. material. But the significance of being accurate about the history is that it confines Bible quotes to those which the pioneers read, learned, and applied (rightly or wrongly) as they sought salvation, cure, and a walk by the spirit the pioneers' own way..

The vice of other approaches is that they frequently are little more than "self-made" A.A. religion, may contain "half baked" prayers, and continue the use "absurd names for God" that have nothing to do with the Twelve Steps as Wilson wrote them or the prior original Bible-based program as Akron developed it. The end result of using these revisionist items leaves the newcomer with conjecture as to what "God's will" actually is, and what "self"will is, and often with confusion on hearing about some nonsense god of someone's own manufacture (such as a rock, a radiator, or a rainbow). Such Biblical creativity may foster an attempted reliance on an untested idolatrous "Biblical" program that may suit the creative writer and the gullible reader, but does not necessarily assure the desired cure of the malady—the curse of alcoholism..

Staying the Course with the One, True, Living God

Believe it or not, there are still doubting Thomases who dispute Dr. Bob's statement that the basic A.A. ideas came from the Bible. Bob either told the truth, or he didn't; and I prefer to think that he did. On the other hand, one or two unbelievers have sought indirectly to put the lie to Dr. Bob's statement by trying to isolate my own research into the Biblical roots of A.A. Supposedly giving credence to their devilish views, they have portrayed as a childish vision and labeled as "infantilism" my 15 years of travel, interviews, investigations at archives and libraries, and reading thousands of books touching on A.A. "spirituality." Using McCarthy-like labeling, one critic distinguishes his views from mine by describing me as a "hobbyist" rather than a scholar (See Ernest Kurtz, *The Collected Ernie Kurtz.* WV: The Bishop of Books, 1999, p. 12). Not content with absurd labels, that same source actually misrepresents my work by alleging that a Californian (yours truly, Dick B.) claims to demonstrate "that every idea in Alcoholics Anonymous derives directly from the King James Version of the Bible" (Kurtz, *supra*, p.17, n.10). If that were the truth, I'd probably shout hurrah, but I leave that canard to those who don't like Californians, Christians, Bible students, active AAs, or doctoral graduates of Western Universities. Poor Leland Stanford would turn over in his grave at such parochial remarks, as would the four United States Supreme Court justices who so recently hailed from Stanford. If there is a view by some from Harvard that Stanford research is childish, represents infantilism, and is at best a hobby, I'll let them wallow in their own name-calling. I'd point out that the Devil is the star accuser and father of lies, and his shenanigans can always be repudiated and trashed by simply relying on spiritual truth.

Yet, however far several non-biblical ideas have led AAs into spiritual confusion, all such A.A. sources, Biblical and non-biblical, sources such as the Bible, Silkworth, Jung, James, Peabody, Buchman, Shoemaker, Anne Smith, Henrietta Seiberling, T. Henry and Clarace Williams, and Emmet Fox, collectively did have an impact on a group of sick people, largely in the Akron alcoholic squad members who turned from religion, church, and medicine to the Bible. Some simple Biblical practices, reliance on God, and Christian Fellowship were used in the successful cures in the 1930's. New Thought, New Age "higher powers," and transcendentalism were hot on their heels, but these forces certainly did not demonstrate a capacity to heal. Only, in my mind, to confuse. And I'm frank to say for the edification of the uninformed or perpetrators of phony labels that many of the revisionist A.A. ideas most certainly did not derive from the Bible.

Like it or not, the remarks and writings of Bill Wilson and Dr. Bob Smith make clear that they were dealing with the one, true, living God—the Creator to whom they so frequently referred, and about whom they studied in the Bible and in their other Christian literature in the 1930's.

7

They could not have escaped hearing or reading: Ephesians 4:6, which taught them there is "One God and Father of all." Acts 2:36 taught that "God hath made that same Jesus, whom ye have crucified, both Lord and Christ." Acts 3: 13 taught that this God was the "God of Abraham, and of Isaac, and of Jacob, the God of our fathers"—descriptions of God that were used by Bill Wilson himself in some writings. 1 Thessalonians 1:9 taught about turning "to God from idols to serve the living and true God." 1 Timothy 4:10 taught: "For therefore we both labour and suffer reproach, because we trust in the living God, who is the Saviour of all men, specially of those who believe." Hebrews 12:22 taught: "But ye are come unto mount Sion, and unto the city of the living God. . ." 1 John 5:20 concludes: "And we know that the Son of God is come, and hath given us an understanding, that we may know him that is true, and we are in him that is true, even in his Son Jesus Christ. This is the true God, and eternal life." These sources represent what the Bible illustrated about the Almighty God that Bill and Bob embraced in framing their talk of the Creator.

In framing his Twelve Steps, Bill Wilson was—in 1938—aiming at the power of the Creator, how to "find" the Creator, and how to "access" the Creator's power. And, through studying the Bible, the early AAs placed their reliance on the one true living God of the Bible and all that the Bible told them about His will, His commandments, His name, His promises, and His plan. When the Big Book was written in 1938, it was never, ever intended to deify what I call the "goofy gods of present-day recovery." Nor was it written to recommend as "Divine Aid" such inanimate "gods" as radiators, chairs, Big Dippers, light bulbs, A.A. itself, Gertrude, and a "higher" power that would be called a "door knob." To the contrary, the basic text was originally supported by Akron people who consistently and continuously asserted that the newcomer must stay the course with the Creator Yahweh, our Almighty God, as he seeks to know and understand Him through the words of the Bible.

Documented Bible sources that were used in connection with basic Step ideas

If you do some deep scratching in our history patch, you can find literature that was widely used in Akron, that mentioned the following Bible verses, and that related them to the problems that newcomers needed to have solved—not the least of which was excessive drinking and resultant alcoholism.

Step One: - "Admission" - Conceding to one's innermost self that something other than medicine would be needed to conquer the demanding, destructive, urge to drink

"O wretched man that I am! who shall deliver me. . ." (Romans 7:22-25)

"Let no man say when he is tempted, I am tempted of God. . ." (James 1:12-16)

"This poor man cried, and the Lord (Yahweh) heard him, and saved him. . ." (Psalm 34:6)

Step Two: - "Belief" - Acknowledging that the "Heavenly Father"— Creator of the heavens and the earth--could and would restore the alcoholic to sanity if He were sought

". . . for he that cometh to God must believe that he is. . ." (Hebrews 11:6)

". . . seek, and ye shall find;" (Mat 7:7; 6:33)

". . . Believe on the Lord Jesus Christ, and thou shalt be saved. . ." (Acts 16:31)

". . . Not every one that saith unto me, Lord, Lord, shall enter into the kingdom of heaven; but he that doeth the will of my Father which is in heaven." (Mat 7:21; 6:10)

"For God hath not given us the spirit of fear; but of power, and of love, and of a sound mind" (2 Tim 1:7)

Step Three: - "Decision" - Doing their Maker's will by turning to Him for care and protection in all areas of life, particularly in resisting the destructive lure of liquor

"But be ye doers of the word, and not hearers only. . ." (James 1:22)

". . . nevertheless not my will, but thine, be done." (Luke 22:42; Mat 6:10)

9

"Trust in the Lord with all thine heart; and lean not unto thine own understanding" (Prov 3:5-6)

Step Four: - "Moral Inventory" - Identifying, listing, and turning from sinful transgressions and progressing with Biblical behavior patterned on the moral standards taught by Jesus

"No man can serve two masters. . . Ye cannot serve God and mammon" (Mat 6:34)

"Thou hypocrite, first cast out the beam out of thine own eye; and then shalt thou see clearly to cast out the mote out of thy brother's eye" (Mat 7:1-5)

"Therefore all things whatsoever ye would that men do to you, do ye even so to them: for this is the law and the prophets" (Mat 7:11-12)

The early yardsticks for self-examination came from Dr. Robert Speer's *Principles of Jesus*, were founded on the essentials for obedience to God's will, and were taught by Jesus: Honesty (John 8:44); Purity (Mat 5:29-30); Unselfishness (Luke 14:33); Love (John 13:34)

The following disobedient behaviors were to be listed, acknowledged, and eliminated: Resentment (Mat 5:21-22, 38-39, 43-44; James 5:9); Self-seeking (James 4:1-6; 1 Cor. 13:4 - 5); Dishonesty (1 Cor 13:4, 6; Phil 4:8); Fear (Mark 5:36; 1 John 4:18); and harming others (James 2:8-13; Numbers 5:6-7; Luke 19:1-10)

Step Five: - "Confession" - The humbling, truthful, admission to God, to another human being, and to yourself the nature of the disobedient acts separating you from a relationship or fellowship with Yahweh, the Creator.

"Confess your faults one to another, and pray for one another, that ye may be healed" (James 5:16)

"If we confess our sins, he is faithful and just to forgive us our sins. . ." (1 John 1:9)

Step Six - "Conviction" - Acknowledging to God your sinful behaviors, admitting to yourself your disobedient actions, and asking Him that they be purged away

"Against thee, thee only have I sinned, and done this evil in thy sight. . ." (Psalm 51:4)

"Iniquities prevail against me: as for our transgressions, thou shalt purge away" (Psalm 51:4)

Step Seven - "Conversion" - The two-fold action by God and by man that seals in the believer the gift of God's spirit once he has obeyed by confessing with his mouth that Jesus is Lord, and believing in his heart that Yahweh, his father, raised Jesus from the dead.

". . . Repent, and be baptized every one of you in the name of Jesus Christ for the remission of sins, and ye shall receive the gift of the Holy Ghost" (Acts 2:38)

"Repent ye therefore, and be converted. . . Unto you first, having raised up his Son Jesus, sent him to bless you, in turning away every one of you from his iniquities" (Acts 3:19)

"Submit yourselves therefore to God. Resist the devil. . ." (James 4:7-8, 10).

". . . And be not conformed to this world; but be ye transformed by the renewing of your mind. . ." (Romans 12:1-2)

Steps Eight and Nine - "Restitution"

"Therefore if any man be in Christ, he is a new creature. . ." (2 Corinthians 5:17).

"Agree with thine adversary quickly. . ." (Mat 5:25)

"If any man say, I love God, and hateth his brother, he is a liar..." (1 John 4:20)

"Therefore if thou bring thy gift to the altar, and there rememberest that thy brother hath ought against thee; Leave there. . . first be reconciled to thy brother. . ." (Mat 5:23-25)

"I will arise and go to my father, and will say unto him, Father, I have sinned against heaven, and before thee. . ." (Luke 15 :18-24)

". . . and if I have taken anything from any man by false accusation, I restore him fourfold. . ." (Luke 19:8-10)

Step Ten - "Continuance" (also called "Conservation") - Recognizing that the new birth has provided forgiveness for sins past; the power to change, the power to overcome evil with good, and the power to do God's will; but that it also requires that the reborn man continue the new life by acting in fellowship with God and with His son Jesus Christ

"Draw nigh to God, and he will draw nigh to you. Cleanse your hands ye sinners. . ." (James 4:8)

"Watch and pray, that ye enter not into temptation: the spirit indeed is willing, but the flesh is weak" (Mat 26:41)

Step Eleven - "Growth through Prayer, Study, and Worship"

"The effectual fervent prayer of a righteous man availeth much" (James 5:16)

"But if we walk in the light, as he is in the light, we have fellowship one with another, and the blood of Jesus Christ his Son cleanseth us from all sin" (1 John 1:7)

"My voice shalt thou hear in the morning, O Lord; in the morning will I direct my prayer unto thee, and will look up" (Psalm 5:3)

"If any of you lack wisdom, let him ask of God. . ." (James 1:5)

"Speak, Lord; for thy servant heareth" (1 Sam 3:9)

"Lord, what wilt thou have me to do" (Acts 9: 6)

"Study to shew thyself approved unto God. . . rightly dividing the word of truth" (2 Tim 2:15)

"Take no thought [be not anxious] about your life, what ye shall eat, or what ye shall drink; nor yet for your body. . . for your heavenly Father knoweth that ye have need of all these things. But seek ye first the kingdom of God, and his righteousness; and all these things shall be added unto you" (Mat 6:25-33)

Step Twelve - "Working with Others"

(a) Awakening to the Power that became available through the new birth:

"But wilt thou know, O vain man, that faith without works is dead" (James 2:20)

"But ye shall receive power, after that the Holy Ghost is come upon you: and ye shall be witnesses unto me. . . unto the uttermost part of the earth" (Acts 1:8)

(b) Telling and helping others with the message of what they can receive:

"Having therefore obtained the help of God, I continue unto this day, witnessing. . ." (Acts 26:22-32)

"Now then we are ambassadors for Christ. . ." (2 Cor 5:20)

"And as ye go, preach, saying, The kingdom of heaven is at hand. Heal the sick, cleanse the lepers, raise the dead, cast out devils: freely ye have received, freely give" (Mat 10:7-8)

(c) Practicing the preaching with love and service while you walk by the spirit.

"Be ye therefore followers of God, as dear children: And walk in love, as Christ also hath loved us, and hath given himself for us. . ." (Ephesians 5:1-2)

"And though I bestow all my goods to feed the poor, and though I give my body to be burned, and have not charity [love], it profiteth me nothing. . ." (1 Cor 13:3-6).

"And whosoever of you will be the chiefest, shall be the servant of all. For even the Son of man came not to be ministered to, but to minister, and to give his life a ransom for many" (Mark 10:43-44).

Part 3:

With the Bible origins in mind, study each step to learn the basic ideas it contains from the Oxford Group

Core Oxford Group Ideas

There have been a number of inadequate, limited descriptions of the core ideas that A.A. borrowed from the Oxford Group. But the picture is not complete unless one realizes that the whole "spiritual program" of A.A., as Bill described it in 1939—and is grounded on the necessity for a "spiritual experience" or "spiritual awakening"—comes almost completely from the Oxford Group's life-changing program. There are some twenty-eight Oxford Group principles that impacted directly on the A.A. program. They are discussed at length in Dick B., *The Oxford Group and Alcoholics Anonymous.* 2d ed., Kihei, HI: Paradise Research Publications, Inc., 1998.

To make them easier to remember and discuss, we have broken the twenty-eight ideas into the following eight segments. Fairly stated, I believe, the following are the eight major groups of ideas:

About God

God is the Creator, Maker, Father, and Almighty. God has a plan. Man's chief end is to conform to that plan. And man starts with the necessity for believing that God *is*. The very expression in A.A.'s Big Book that "God either is or He isn't" came almost verbatim from the writings of Oxford Group leader Reverend Sam Shoemaker. Rev. Shoemaker and early A.A. were each emphatic in their written suggestions that *suffering people need to find God now*.

About Sin

The Oxford Group had a simple description for sin: Sin was whatever blocked a person from God and from other people. Sin was also defined as selfishness, self-centeredness, ego-centricity, the big "I." All are terms well known to AAs. Sin, said the Oxford Group, had to be eliminated in order for man to have a relationship with God. The formula for eliminating sin could be described in two different ways. The first description came from Frank Buchman: Sin is the problem Jesus Christ is the cure, and the result is A Miracle. The second description came from what Buchman called "God's art." It required acting on Buchman's ideas of Surrender, Soul Surgery (to cut away and eliminate the sin), and the result—a changed or transformed life.

Eliminating Sin through Self-Surrender

There is a "turning point" in A.A., (Its language is expressed so frequently in Sam Shoemaker's writings, and in the Oxford Group's life-changing program). And turning point is a phrase picked up from the following quote from Professor William James, the much admired Harvard psychologist from whom Bill Wilson borrowed a few A.A. ideas— actually probably taken from Shoemaker's remarks about James. Shoemaker described the "turning point" as follows:

> Self-surrender has always been and always must be regarded as the vital turning point of the religious life, so far as the religious life is spiritual and no affair of outer works and ritual and sacraments. One may say that the whole development of Christianity in inwardness has consisted in little more than the greater and greater emphasis attached to this crisis of self-surrender (Samuel M. Shoemaker, Jr. *Realizing Religion*, NY: The Association Press, 1921, p. 30).

The Power through Jesus Christ

People cannot change themselves, said the Oxford Group. The transforming power of Jesus Christ that is gained through being born again of the spirit is absolutely essential. Men and women surrender. They do this by believing in God, seeking God first, and being transformed, born again of the spirit of God. At the beginning of their life-changing decision, many in the Oxford Group epitomized their surrenders with the simple prayer: "Thy will be done"—from the Lord's prayer in the Sermon on the Mount.

The Life-Changing Five C's

Mankind has a role in establishing the relationship with God. As Shoemaker put it, people suffer from spiritual misery because there is estrangement from God by people who were meant to be His companions. You need a vital religious experience; you need to find God; you need Jesus Christ, said Shoemaker in *Realizing Religion, supra*, p. 9. The "art" of changing lives by eliminating sin, said Frank Buchman, could be described in terms of Five C's—Confidence, Confession, Conviction, Conversion, and Continuance (Harold Begbie, *Life Changers*. London: Mills and Boon, Ltd, 1932, p. 169).

These five ideas were mentioned in early A.A. and formed the heart of its middle Steps (Three through Eleven). Confidence meant gaining the confidence of a newcomer through witnessing and the mutual sharing of one's innermost secrets by the life-changer and the new person. The confidential sharing was generated in the second "C" (the actual Confession of sins or shortcomings). Conviction meant that the new person acknowledged that the confessed faults and shortcomings were sins against the ways of God and therefore needed to be eliminated before "conscious contact" with God could occur. Conversion was the instrument of change. It involved submission to God, humbly throwing one's self on the mercy of God, and then, by His grace, becoming His children through a new birth—"Christ in you." Finally, there was "Conservation" or "Continuance" which meant continued daily contact with God (involving inventory, confession, conviction, and restitution), communication with God in Quiet Times, experiencing His deliverance, witnessing to others about that deliverance, and obediently practicing God's own spiritual principles. Those principles were often simply described by Dr. Bob as "love and service." These were the watch-word principles stressed in, and part of his youthful learning as, a Christian Endeavorer in St. Johnsbury, Vermont.

Restitution or Amends

Especially unique in the A.A. program and in the life-changing practices of its Oxford Group precursor, was the enormous emphasis on making restitution for harms done. The Oxford Group writings listed several Bible segments in support of the idea. But the foundational Bible source was to be found in the Sermon on the Mount (Matthew 5:23-26). There Jesus taught that where there was controversy, there was a duty to agree with one's adversary quickly and then to clear up the wreckage of the past. This was God's will, said the Oxford Group; and carrying that principle out was essential to a new relationship with God and with others. The Big Book used virtually the same words on the last page of its basic text (p. 164).

Daily Surrender

Some forget the emphasis the Oxford Group placed on *daily* watchfulness and rectification. Bill Wilson added this practice (that derived from the Oxford Group's "continuance") to the supposed original six word-of-mouth steps. He placed this requirement in Step Ten. There was to be a daily watchfulness for sin, a daily confession to others, a daily conviction and turning to God for help, a daily making of amends, and a daily concern for helping others. Love and tolerance were A.A.'s declared code, The two code items were Biblical, Christian Endeavor, and Oxford Group ideas.

Quiet Time

Little needs to be repeated here about the elements of Quiet Time. But daily contact with God was a major part of Oxford Group life and spiritual growth. The daily turning to God was placed by Wilson in the Eleventh Step. In the Oxford Group and in early A.A., Quiet Time meant Bible study, use of helpful religious books, prayer, listening to God's direction, writing down thoughts, checking them, and, of course, obeying them. The persistence of these original Quiet Time ideas in A.A. is manifested by Dr. Bob's firm endorsement of them in his last major address to AAs in 1948 (*The Co-Founders of Alcoholics Anonymous*, pp. 11-14, 16-18).

Spiritual Awakening, Witness, Practice of Principles

The A.A. terms "spiritual awakening" and "spiritual experience" came straight from the frequent use of those terms by Oxford Group Founder Dr. Frank Buchman, by Rev. Sam Shoemaker, and by many other Oxford Group writers. The terms had to do with attaining "God-consciousness"—a term also mentioned with frequency in the Oxford Group and early A.A.

After the "awakening," witnessing to what God had done for you (or "sharing for witness" as the Group called it) was a vital part of the new spiritual life. And "passing it on" was one phrase that described witnessing. The idea was Biblical; and Frank Buchman and other Oxford

Group people referred to this very idea in the expression—"pass it on." Jesus Christ definitely emphasized the idea of witness (Mark 16:10-10). Frank Buchman actually used the term "pass it on" (Buchman, *Remaking the World*, 1961, p. x). And Rev. Sam Shoemaker frequently said: "You have to give it away to keep it"—a term well known in A.A.

Practicing spiritual principles was the last part of the new life. And the definition of the spiritual principles focused on the Oxford Group's Four Absolutes—honesty, purity, unselfishness and love. These Four Absolutes or Four Standards are still mentioned in the Oxford Group today, and also in various parts of A.A. Also incorporated in the principles to be practiced were the "love" ingredients set forth in1 Corinthians 13 and stressed by Professor Henry Drummond in his little book "The Greatest Thing in the World."

Specific Oxford Group Ideas in the Twelve Steps

Step One

"O, God, manage me, because I cannot manage myself." This simple prayer was often mentioned by Frank Buchman, Sam Shoemaker, and Anne Smith. Its counter-part can be found in A.A.'s "Our lives had become unmanageable."

Step Two

Sam Shoemaker wrote of the need for "a Force outside himself, greater than himself" and "a vast Power outside themselves." He insisted that there be a willingness to believe, and that there be a belief in God. The willingness, he said, was wrapped up in the experiment of faith by which a person stepped out on the belief by obeying God and realizing, as Jesus taught in John 7:17, that the believing produced results because it the expected results were based on God's promises.

Step Three

The Oxford Group laid the foundation for the A.A. idea that surrender starts with a *decision*. Sam Shoemaker's *Twice-Born Ministers* described that decision (Samuel M. Shoemaker, Jr. *Twice-Born Ministers*. NY: Fleming H. Revell, 1929). He used language that Bill Wilson borrowed almost verbatim for A.A.'s Step Three. Shoemaker wrote of: "the decision to cast my will and my life on God" (p.34). Shoemaker also pre-empted and virtually framed the famous A.A. expression "God as we understood Him." He frequently spoke of "surrendering as much of yourself as you understand to as much of God as you understand" (Samuel M. Shoemaker, *Children of the Second Birth* NY: Fleming H. Revell,

1927, pp. 27, 47). Then, using language similar to that later adopted in A.A.'s original Third Step draft, Shoemaker said: "She surrendered to God . . . and . . . turned over to Him her life for His direction" (*Children of the Second Birth*, p. 82).

Step Four

The language of Step Four is Oxford Group. In *Soul Surgery*, Oxford Group writer H. A. Walter pointed to Frank Buchman's insistence that each person "make the moral test" (Howard A. Walter, *Soul-Surgery*. Calcutta: Association Press, 1919, pp. 43-44). Oxford Group mentor Henry Drummond wrote that man needs to "devote his soul to self-examination, to self-examination of the most solemn and searching kind" (Henry Drummond. *The Ideal Life*, NY: Hodder and Stoughton, 1897 p. 316). Frank Buchman said: "Moral recovery starts when everyone admits his own faults instead of spot-lighting the other fellow's" (Frank N. D. Buchman, *Remaking the World*, London: Blandford Press, 1961, p. 46). The examination was in terms of how well one was living up to the four standards—honesty, purity, unselfishness, and love.

Step Five

Oxford Group writer Stephen Foot explained as to confession: "The first step for me was to be honest with God, the next to be honest with men" (Stephen Foot, *Life Began Yesterday*, NY: Harper and Brothers, 1935, p. 11). Howard Walter wrote: "Be ready to confess your own shortcomings honestly and humbly" (Walter, *Soul Surgery*, *supra*, p. 57).

Step Six

In *The Venture of Belief,* Oxford Group activist Philip Marshall Brown wrote: "To summarize the various stages of spiritual adventure; first, the will to believe; second, the honest facing and sharing of all conscious sin; third, the complete surrender of self to God; and, fourth, the willingness to obey His will" (Philip M. Brown, *The Venture of Belief*, NY: Fleming H. Revell, 1935, p. 36). This willingness was underlined by a conviction of sin and the need to repent.

Step Seven

In *I Was a Pagan*, Bill Wilson's friend and Oxford Group co-worker Victor Kitchen wrote: "It takes the power of God to remove the desire for these indulgences" (Victor C. Kitchen, *I Was a Pagan*, NY: Harper Brothers, 1935, p. 143). Kitchen also said: "I then and there admitted my inability to quit of my own will and asked God to take charge of the matter" (p. 74). He also said: "God . . . satisfied unsound desire by removing the desire itself" (p. 73).

Step Eight

"God cannot take over my life unless I am willing," said Cecil Rose in *When Man Listens* (NY: Oxford University Press, 1937, p. 17). Oxford Group writer Jack Winslow said: "A further point in the moral challenge which the Oxford Group presents is that known as restitution, viz. putting right, as far as in our power, wrongs committed in the past" (Jack Winslow, *Why I Believe in the Oxford Group*, London: Hodder & Stoughton, 1934, p. 31).

Step Nine

Cecil Rose said: "These first steps of restitution are absolutely necessary if I am to start the new life clear with God and other people. . . . [The] great task that is waiting: cooperate with God and to ask God to make us fit for Him to use" (Rose, *When Man Listens, supra*, p. 20).

Step Ten

Shoemaker said: "There is need for rededication day by day, hour by hour, by which progressively, in every Quiet Time, the contaminations of sin and self-will are further sloughed off, for they do have a way of collecting" (Samuel M. Shoemaker, Jr., *The Conversion of the Church*, NY: Fleming H. Revell, 1932, p.79). And using language which A.A. seems to have adopted verbatim, Frank Buchman said: "What is the disease? Isn't it fear, dishonesty, resentment, selfishness?" (Buchman, *Remaking the World, supra*, p. 38). In Steps 10 and 11, Wilson specifically mentioned these shortcomings as those requiring continued watchfulness.

Step Eleven

Philip M. Brown wrote: "They tell of the strength of heart and mind, of the depth of knowledge of life, of the charity and love that are poured into human beings whenever they establish contact with God" (Brown, *The Venture of Belief, supra*, p. 24). Stephen Foot said: (1) "Contact with God is the necessary fundamental condition, and that is made through prayer and listening. . . ." (2) "I will ask God to show me His purpose for my life and claim from Him the power to carry that purpose out" (Foot, *Life Began Yesterday, supra*, pp. 13, 11). Victor Kitchen wrote: "I 'emerged' into God-consciousness" (Kitchen, *I Was a Pagan, supra*, p. 43).

Step Twelve

(a) As to an awakening, Walter wrote in Soul Surgery: "The basis of conversion is the awakening of a new self, and the vital element in this new birth is the dawning of a new affection which dominates the heart" (Walter, Soul Surgery, supra, p. 82). Sam Shoemaker said: "This experience, which I consider was my conversion, brought to me a new kind of life which was entirely new to me" (Shoemaker, Twice-Born Ministers, supra, p. 55). (b) As to sharing the experience, long ago, Frank Buchman wrote: "The best way to keep an experience of Christ is to pass it on" (Buchman, Remaking the World, supra, p. x). (c) As to practicing the principles taught in the Sermon on the Mount and elsewhere in the Bible, A. J. Russell wrote: "Moreover, it meant a relentless crusade to induce other men and women not only to believe in the possibility of living the victorious life, but to live it" (A. J. Russell, For Sinners Only, London: Hodder & Stoughton, 1932, p. 62). B. H. Streeter wrote in The God Who Speaks: "Christ does not merely teach men what to do, he gives them power to do it" (Streeter, The God Who Speaks, p. 151).

Part 4:

Once you have learned the Bible sources and the Oxford Group ideas, then study each Step, observing how closely it parallels the language of America's OG leader, Sam Shoemaker

Specific Shoemaker Ideas in A.A.

Every AA who stays in our fellowship long enough to be exposed to its Big Book, its Twelve Steps, and its meeting buzzwords will readily recognize here thoughts that seem to have come directly from the books and other writings of Sam Shoemaker.

These include: (1) Self-surrender. (2) Self is not God. (3) God either is, or He isn't. (4) "Turning point." (5) Conversion. (6) Prayer. (7) Fellowship. (8) Willingness. (9) Self-examination. (10) Confession of faults to God, self, and another. (11) Amends. (12) "Thy will be done." (13) Spiritual Experience. (14) Spiritual Awakening. (15) The unmanageable life. (16) Power greater than ourselves. (17) God as you understand Him. (18) The "Four Absolutes"-- honesty, purity, unselfishness, and love. (19) Guidance of God. (20) "Faith without works is dead." (21) "Love thy neighbor as thyself." (22) References to Almighty God (using Bible terms) as our "Creator," "Maker," "Father," "Spirit," "God of our fathers," and "Father of Lights." (23) The Lord's Prayer. (24) Jesus's "sermon on the mount." (25) Self-centeredness. (26) Fear. (27) Grudges. (28) Quiet Time. (29) Reliance on God. (30) Relationship with God. (31) "Giving it away to keep it." (32) "News, not views." (33) God has a plan. (34) Seeking God first. (35) Belief in God. (36) Born again. (37) Marvel at what God has done for you. (38) Let go! (39) Abandon yourself to Him [God]. (40) "Not my will but Thine be done." And many others.

You can find, in my title "New Light on Alcoholism," a list of 149 Shoemaker expressions that very closely parallel A.A. language. Many more can be found in specific quotations from Shoemaker's books, books which have been fully reviewed in Dick B., New Light on Alcoholism: God, Sam Shoemaker, and A.A., 2d ed. (http://www.dickb.com/newlight.shtml).

Shoemaker and the individual Twelve Steps

Make no mistake. Whatever Bill Wilson may have said or implied from time to time, Sam Shoemaker was **not** the only source of A.A.'s spiritual ideas. Wilson often pointed his applause in Sam's direction in an effort to avoid Roman Catholic and other objections to the Oxford Group from which A.A.'s ideas also came and of which early A.A. was a part. Moreover, Bill never mentioned with attribution the A.A. specifics that came from Dr. Bob, Anne Smith, the Bible, Quiet Time, God's direct guidance or Christian literature that was daily fare in early A.A.

Remember also! Dr. Bob said he did not write the Twelve Steps and had nothing to do with writing them. Those Steps supposedly represented Bill's personal interpretation of, and inspiration from, the spiritual program that had been in progress since 1935. Bill's language much more resembled Shoemaker's language and Oxford Group ideas (that Ebby Thacher had learned from the Oxford Group and passed on to Bill in New York). Dr. Bob emphasized, on more than one occasion, that A.A.'s basic ideas had come from study of the Bible. Dr. Bob never said that about either the Oxford Group or Shoemaker. Dr. Bob studied the Bible. Daily, for three months, Anne Smith read the Bible to Bill and Bob. Bob read the Bible to AAs. He quoted the Bible to AAs. He gave them Bible literature. And he frequently stressed Bible study, stating that the Book of James, 1 Corinthians 13, and Jesus's Sermon on the Mount (Matthew 5 to 7) were considered absolutely essential in the early spiritual recovery program. Bill Wilson and Dr. Bob both said that the Sermon on the Mount contained the underlying philosophy of A.A.

But Sam's own imprint is nonetheless on the Steps. Every one of them. His imprint was on the presentation of Oxford Group ideas that Ebby Thacher made to Bill Wilson in Towns Hospital. And we will briefly take a look at just where Shoemaker's language parallels the language of the Twelve Steps. In fact, our third chapter in *New Light on Alcoholism* provides further details and complete documentation.

Step One: Shoemaker spoke of the gap between man and God which man is **powerless** to bridge, man having lost the power to deal with sin for himself. As to the **unmanageable life**, Sam referred to the prayer in the Oxford Group so often described in Frank Buchman's tale of "Victor's Story" and quoted by Anne Smith in her journal: "God manage me, because I can't manage myself."

Step Two: Sam spelled out the need for a **power greater than ourselves**. He quoted Hebrews 11:6 for the proposition that **God is.** He declared: God is God, and **self is not God**; and man must so believe. Sam urged **seeking God first**, from Matthew 6:33. He espoused the "experiment of faith" by which man **believes** that God is; **seeks** God first in his actions, and then **knows** God **by doing** God's will, and then can acknowledging and seeing that God provides the needed and promised power. For this idea, Sam frequently cited John 7:17.

Step Three: Sam taught that **self-surrender is the vital turning-point of the religious life**, and quoted from William James's *The Varieties of Religious Experience*, NY: First Vintage Books/The Library of America Edition, 1990, p. 106. Sam said this turning point involved being **born again of the spirit of God.** He declared that man must make a **decision** to renounce sins, **accept Jesus Christ as Saviour; and begin Christian life** in earnest. Sam illustrated a surrender using language similar to that in A.A.'s Third Step. Sam spoke of a "decision to cast my will and my life on God." Many times, Sam said one need only surrender as much of himself as he understands to **as much of God as he understands**. A clear precursor of A.A.'s "God as we understood Him"–which has unfortunately been misunderstood and has been attributed to other sources.

Step Four: Sam wrote of **self-examination** to find where one's life fell short of the **Four Absolute Standards of Jesus: honesty, purity, unselfishness, and love**. One was to **write down** exactly where he had "fallen short." There was a "**moral obligation**" to face these facts, recognize these as blocks to God, and be "**ruthlessly, realistically honest.**"

Step Five: Shoemaker taught of **honesty with self and honesty with God, quoted James 5:16 for the importance of confession to others, and stressed the need for detailed sharing of, and honestly owning up to one's darkest secrets**.

Step Six: Though the fact of Bill's borrowing of this "**conviction**" step from the Oxford Group 5 C's seems to have been overlooked,

Shoemaker taught often about the need for man's conviction that he has been miserable, has (by his sins) become estranged from God, and needs to come back to God in honest penitence. Sam urged **willingness to ask God** to show exactly where one is failing and then to give him strength admit that sin.

Step Seven: Sam clarified this as the "**conversion**" step of the 5 C's. It meant a **new birth**, he said. It meant **humility**. It meant, for Shoemaker, the **assumption upon ourselves of God's will for us and the opening of ourselves to receiving the "grace of God which alone converts."** It meant "**drawing near and putting ourselves in position to be converted. . . utter dedication to the will of God**." Shoemaker often defined "sin" as that which blocks us from God and from others." So, originally, did Big Book language. And each of the foregoing life-changing steps hangs on early A.A.'s definition of sin and the "removal" process of examining for sin, confessing sin, becoming convicted of sin, and becoming converted through surrendering it. The conversion experience, according to Shoemaker and early A.A., established or enabled rediscovery of a "relationship with God" and initiated the new life that developed from the relationship with God which conversion opened. Both the Sixth and Seventh Steps were new to A.A. thinking. They added something to the original "surrenders" to Jesus Christ. And I believe these Steps Six and Seven cannot easily be understood at all without seeing them in terms of the complete surrender, the new relationship, the new birth, and the giving of the sins to God for pardon-- as Shoemaker saw the process and as Bill attempted to write it into the recovery path.

Step Eight: Wilson added this additional step to the Oxford Group's "restitution" practice. In so doing, Bill focused again on Shoemaker's talk of "**willingness**"--stemming from John 7:17. In Step Six, it was willingness to ask **God's help** in removing the blocks. Then, in Step Eight, it was willingness to be convicted of the need to make restitution and to go "**to someone with restoration and apology**."

Step Nine: Sam said the last stand of self is **pride.** There can be no talk of humility, he said, until **pride licks the dust**, and one then **acts to make full restoration and restitution for wrongs done**. As AAs in Akron usually quoted from the Sermon on the Mount to justify amends, Sam also quoted those sermon verses enjoining the bringing of a gift to the altar without first being reconciled to one's brother (**Matthew 5:22-24**). Restitution was not merely a good deed to be done. It implemented

God's command in the Bible that wrongs be righted as part of the practicing the principle of love. If one understands Shoemaker, one can understand the absurdity of some present-day AAs' guilt-ridden suggestions that one can make an amend to a dead person by writing a letter to the deceased or by volunteering help for the down-trodden or by making a substitutionary gift to some worthy cause. **Sam taught that the required amends were not merely about "works." They were about empowered and guided love in action!**

Step Ten: This step concerned **daily surrender** and the Oxford Group idea of "**continuance**." Sam taught that, in addition to making an initial surrender to God, it was **necessary to continue** self-examination, confession, conviction, the seeking of God's help, and the prompt making of amends. This continued action was to follow through on the new relationship with God and others that followed the initial forgiveness of sin that occurred through the new birth in the earlier steps.

Step Eleven: Sam wrote eloquently about **Quiet Time, Bible study, prayer, and "meditation"** (listening for God's guidance). Sam urged daily contact with God for **guidance, forgiveness, strength, and spiritual growth**. So does A.A.'s Big Book. Quiet Time was a "must" in early A.A. And Shoemaker defined every aspect of Quiet Time from the necessity for a new birth to a new willingness to study, pray, listen, and read rather than to speak first and lead with the chin. "Speak Lord for thy servant heareth" was one of Sam's favored verses for describing the posture of Quiet Time. So also, said Sam, was Paul's plea in the Book of Acts, "What shall I do Lord?"

Step Twelve: This step comprehends three major A.A./Shoemaker ideas:

(1) **A spiritual awakening**, the exact meaning of which Shoemaker spelled out in his books and in his talks to AAs. Sam declared that a spiritual awakening consisted of (a) conversion, (b) prayer, (c) fellowship, and (d) witness.

(2) **A witnessing message telling what God has done for us that we were unable to accomplish for ourselves.** Shoemaker epitomized the task by saying, in several ways: "**You have to give Christianity away to keep it**." Sam's "you have to give it away to keep it" has become a part of A.A. shop-talk and was incorporated in one of the Big Book personal

stories that spoke of the four A.A. paradoxes: You have to give it away to keep it; you have to surrender to win, etc.

(3) **Practicing the new design for living by walking in harmony with God's will with love and service toward others.** Bill originally phrased this third idea in terms of helping other alcoholics without charge. But it appears that the whole segment was broadened into language easily recognized in Sam's teachings—declaring that a real spiritual awakening means there has been a conversion, that there is continued prayer, that there is fellowship with like-minded believers, that witnessing to the gospel message concerns the availability of God's grace and power, and proof that the message carrier is practicing God's principles as defined in the Bible.

The Twelfth Step language; its vague phrases like awakening and message and principles; and its lack of specificity about those elements, illustrates the importance of Shoemaker's teachings and their ultimate, yet obscure home in A.A. Bill's Twelfth Step language. Bill's words—lacking as they do the explanatory origins from Sam—have become ill-defined and illusory. Any A.A. Big Book student knows how skimpy and inadequate the three Big Book Twelfth Step ideas are treated in the text itself..

Neither the Twelfth Step language nor the accompanying chapter in the Big Book sets forth or explains what an awakening is, what the message is, or what the principles are. To be frank, we know that present-day A.A. has left Christianity in the dust. In so doing, AAs lost in their Twelfth Step an understanding of what Sam Shoemaker taught, Dr. Bob emphasized, and Sam meant prior to the writings in which Bill emasculated the material. Conversion, the gospel message, and practicing love and service are all a part of early A.A. history and successes. They are all clearly defined in the **Book of Acts, the Four Absolutes, 1 Corinthians 13, Jesus' Sermon on the Mount, the Book of James, and other specific parts of the Bible.** Therefore, if you want to know the subject matter that Bill covered so confusingly and inadequately in his Twelfth Step language, you will want to study Shoemaker's role, teaching, and writings and the part these played in Bill's intended message.

28

Part 5:

A much better understanding of each of the steps can then be gained by seeing how much of the Bible material, Oxford Group ideas, and Shoemaker writings were being taught in early A.A. in Anne Smith's (Dr. Bob's Wife's) writings

Anne Smith's Spiritual Journal, 1933-1939

From the earliest years of A.A.'s beginnings in Akron, Anne Smith assembled, compiled, and shared with AAs and their families each morning at the Smith home the contents of her spiritual journal. Of Anne's service, Akron old timer John R. said:

> Before one of these meetings [in Dr. Bob's home], Anne used to pull out a little book [her spiritual journal] and quote from it. We would discuss it. Then we would see what Anne would suggest from it for our discussion (Dick B. *The Akron Genesis of Alcoholics Anonymous*, 2d ed. Kihei, HI: Paradise Research Publications, Inc., 1998, p. 110).

Anne's journal has lain virtually unstudied, despite the existence of copies in the A.A. Archives in New York and at Bill Wilson's home at Stepping Stones. Yet it is priceless in the information it supplies, the ideas it propounds, and the history it records. It was kept by Anne in her own hand and partly typed up for her by her daughter Sue Smith Windows. It covers Anne's notes about the Bible, the Oxford Group, the literature AAs read, and almost every Step idea that was later adopted and placed in the Big Book in 1939. Why, then, has this important historical information source been ignored!

Almost all of what we cover here comes directly from the contents of Anne's journal itself, but one cannot see the full picture without studying our report of it in *Anne Smith's Journal, 1933-1939*, 3rd ed. (Kihei, HI: Paradise Research Publications, Inc., 1998).

Anne and the Twelve Step Ideas

If, in the summer of 1935 at the Smith home in Akron, Bill and Bob were developing the Twelve Step ideas, Anne was certainly learning them, recording them, or recording them. And probably all three. While we will not cover material already set forth in our parts about the Bible, the Oxford Group, and Shoemaker, we need to sketch out the Step ideas as Anne expressed them—before there was any Big Book and before Bill had written the Steps in December of 1938. This because they are so directly linked to what Bill and Bob were doing and saying as they developed the spiritual program of recovery in the home of Dr. Bob and Anne Smith and also to what all three people were absorbing from Oxford Group literature and activists like T. Henry Williams, Eleanor Forde, and Rev. Sam Shoemaker. Even Henrietta Seiberling, though new on board.

Step One. Anne twice specifically mentioned **the "manage me" prayer** that was popular with Buchman and Shoemaker ("O Lord manage me, for I cannot manage myself").

Step Two. Using language resembling that in A.A.'s Second Step, Anne said: "A **stronger power than his was needed**. God provided the power through Christ, so that we could find a new relationship with God."

Step Three. "Try to bring a person to **a decision to 'surrender as much of himself as he knows to as much of God as he knows.'** Stay with him until he makes a decision and says it out loud." She added, "Surrender is a complete handing over of our wills to God, a reckless abandon of ourselves, all that we have, all that we think, that we are, everything we hold dear, to God to do what he likes with. . . ."

Step Four. "It is absolutely necessary to face people with **the moral test**. . . . Criticism born of my own projection. Something wrong in me. Unless I can crystalize the criticism, I had better look for the mote in my eye. . . . Make the moral test. **4 Standards** [the Four Absolutes]. . . . Why I had been absolutely honest but not living [it]. . . . Resentments to be faced and set right. . . . Fear and worry are atheism. . . . Just a glimpse of self-centered life."

Step Five. "Confess your faults one to another. . . . I must share to be **honest with God, myself & others."**

Step Six. "**Be willing** to ask God where I am failing and to **admit sin**."

Step Seven. [Speaking of sins such as selfishness, dishonesty, and pride, Anne wrote:] **"Christ can only remove them and replace with a new quality of life**. Read Romans 12. . . . Do not pretend you can go on lifting yourself by your own boot straps. In all humility to God, "What would thou have me to do?". . . . I'm wrong, Father. . . **show me the way."**

Steps Eight and Nine. "Any restitution I won't make. . . . Resentments to be faced and set right. . . . **Restitution** to be made. . . . Help them make a **list** of things. . . . God can make me **willing** in the day of His power."

Step Ten. "Check your life constantly by the four absolutes." "Our lives will be one continuous surrender: surrender to God of every difficulty that confronts us, each temptation, each spiritual struggle, laying before Him either to take away or to show us in their proper spiritual proportions." "Be willing to ask God where I am failing and to admit sin."

Step Eleven. (1) *Prayer*: "Intercessory prayer—pray that Spirit may tell you what to pray for. . . . A way to find God's will not to change it." "Petitionary prayers. . . . These we submit not because we distrust His goodness or desire to bend His Will but because He is our Friend. . . . Correct me—direct—praise—adoration and thanksgiving. Romans II." (2) *Guidance*: "Guidance is the principle of the Bible, its very structure." "We must be in such relationship with God that He can guide us. . . . Specifically, guidance comes through intelligent knowledge of the Bible, through conscience, through circumstance. . . . guidance is thinking plus God." "I will lead you and guide you in all truth, and bring all thoughts to your remembrance (John)." (3) *Listening*: "Watch your thoughts. Your thoughts can come from three sources. 1. Subconscious. 2. The devil. 3. God." (4) *Bible study and reading*: "Let all your reading be guided. . . . Of course the Bible ought to be the main Source Book of all." (5) *Quiet Time*: "Effective Quiet Time: 1. Objective, God and obedience. 2. Attentive prayer and being willing to act immediately. 3. Stillness and surrender of all known sins."

In addition, there are many many specific comments about prayer, listening, reading, and the like that should be read to get the full flavor and depth of Anne's teaching.

Step Twelve. (1) *Having had a spiritual experience*: **"A general experience of God is the first essential,** the beginning. We can't give away what we haven't got. We must have a genuine contact with God in our present experience." (2) *Carrying the message*: **"Giving Christianity away is the best way to keep it."** "When we have that [a general experience of God], witnessing to it is natural, just as we want to share a beautiful sunset." (3) *Practicing the principles*: **"Start the person on a new life with simple, concrete and definite suggestions, regarding Bible study, prayer, overcoming temptation and service to others**." "God's answer to materialism is a basis of Christian living that lifts above material things." "Claim from **God humility, patience, courage, faith and love."**

For the specifics and page numbers in this journal kept by Dr. Bob's wife and shared with early AAs and their families, see Dick B. *Anne Smith's Journal*, 1933-1939, 3rd ed. Kihei, HI: Paradise Research Publications, Inc., 1998.

Part 6:

Read carefully this study and critique of what Bill claimed were six steps—six "word-of-mouth" ideas already in place

A careful student of our Twelve Step origins will view with caution the allegations of Bill Wilson and even his wife Lois that there were some "six" steps—supposedly from the Oxford Group—that were "word-of-mouth" ideas being utilized before the Twelve Steps were written. Of course, that may have been Bill's sincere perception of what he was doing. But his descriptions varied immensely. There were no Oxford Group steps at all. And, with one exception, there is no evidence that Dr. Bob varied from the "James Club" emphasis on James, the Sermon, and 1 Corinthians and instead was using these six ideas. Finally, they do not fit with the precise description of the Akron program that Rockefeller's agent Frank Amos investigated and reported before Bill ever began writing the Big Book. For what they are worth, however, here are the details.

Comparing varied statements of and about early A.A.'s alleged "Six Steps"

1. A common rendition: Bill Wilson made the following record of his thoughts, as he prepared, in December of 1938, to write the Twelve Steps:

> "Though subject to considerable variation, it [the "word of mouth program"] boiled down into a pretty consistent procedure which comprised six steps. These were approximately as follows:
>
> 1. We admitted that we were licked, that we were powerless over alcohol.
> 2. We made a moral inventory of our defects or sins.
> 3. We confessed or shared our shortcomings with another person in confidence.

4. We made restitution to all those we had harmed by our drinking.
5. We tried to help other alcoholics, with no thought of reward in money or prestige.
6. We prayed to whatever God we thought there was for power to practice these precepts.

This was the substance of what, by the fall of 1938, we were telling newcomers."[1]1

2. A probable earlier rendition by Bill in his own words: Of another and possibly earlier time, Bill wrote as follows in a *Grapevine* article:

"As we commenced to form a Society separate from the Oxford Group, we began to state our principles something like this:

1. We admitted we were powerless over alcohol [part of present-day Step One language, but not the language of the Oxford Group, Bible, or Bob].

2. We got honest with ourselves [part of the Step One admission idea and the Step Four moral inventory concept].

3. We got honest with another person, in confidence [Part of the Step Five confession concept, but leaves out Oxford Group's "God, ourselves, and another person"].

4. We made amends for harms done others [the 8th and 9th Step ideas about restitution].

5. We worked with other alcoholics without demand for prestige or money [Part of the Step 12 idea, but omits the message and the principles such as giving it away to keep it and living by the Four Absolutes and other Christian principles].

6. We prayed to God to help us to do these things as best we could [A much abbreviated description of Quiet Time, Bible study, devotionals, and guidance with a limited description of 11th and 12th Step ideas]."[2]

---

1. [1]*AA Comes of Age*, NY: Alcoholics Anonymous World Services, In., p. 160.
   [2]*The Language of the Heart*, NY: The AA Grapevine, Inc., p. 200.

3. A possible input from Bill's wife: Lois Wilson described "the Oxford Group precepts" as:

> "1. Surrender your life to God. [Step 3 and Oxford Group ideas]
>
> 2. Take a moral inventory. [Step 4 and Oxford Group idea]
>
> 3. Confess your sins to God and another human being. [Step 5, Oxford Group, Bible ideas]
>
> 4. Make restitution. [Steps 8 and 9, Oxford Group, and Bible ideas]
>
> 5. Give of yourself to others with no demand for return [Eliminates awakening, witness, and practice of principles, which were all Oxford Group ideas].
> 6. Pray to God for help to carry out these principles." [Part 11 and 12 ideas][3]

---

[3]*Lois Remembers* (New York: Al-Anon Family Group Headquarters, 1987), p. 92. But A.A.'s *Pass It On* contains this statement in Footnote 2 on page 206: "In later years, some A.A. members referred to this procedure as the six steps of the Oxford Group. Reverend T. Willard Hunter, who spent 18 years in full-time staff positions for the Oxford Group and M.R.A., said, 'I never once saw or heard anything like the Six Tenets. It would be impossible to find them in any Oxford Group-M.R.A. literature. I think they must have been written by someone else under some sort of misapprehension.'" In the past two years, I have heard statements that A.A.'s six steps came from the "six steps of the Oxford Group." After reviewing thousands of pages of Oxford Group-Shoemaker writings, I have found no reference to such six steps or six tenets. However, Lois's summary does comprehend *six of some twenty-eight* principles I found in Oxford Group-Shoemaker writings. See Dick B., *The Oxford Group and Alcoholics Anonymous*, 2d ed. And, the "licked," "powerless," and "deflation" ideas do bear some resemblance to the countless stories in Oxford Group-Shoemaker writings that start with the helpless, hopeless condition of some "twice-born" person before he had his religious experience; and Shoemaker does speak of "spiritual misery," the "unhappiness of spiritual people," and the spiritual "malady" which is "estrangement from God." See Samuel M. Shoemaker, *Realizing Religion* (New York: Association Press, 1923), pp. 4-5. This spiritual problem prompted Shoemaker to say, "What you want is simply a vital religious experience. You need to find God. You need Jesus Christ" (p. 9). The concept of "estrangement from God" is not only biblical, but is frequently found in the Oxford Group-Shoemaker writings. However, Lois's characterization of a supposed six Oxford Group steps at least shows her perception of, and accuracy in, describing six of some of the many twenty-eight Oxford Group ideas that impacted A.A Actually, Lois' words portray the Oxford Group ideas more specifically and with more care than Bill used when he talked about the same ideas. No matter what Lois or Bill or Earl T. may have said, we can confirm and agree with Rev. Willard Hunter's expert and informed opinion that there were no spinoff steps or tenets, "six in number," in the Oxford Group. No grouping at all of these six ideas as steps or as a program under the Oxford Group banner. Moreover, there is no mention of six steps in the A.A. program except for the excerpt from Earl Treat, the "word-of-mouth" variants by Bill Wilson. And Dr. Bob plainly said that there were no steps at all.

4. An alleged version attributed to Dr. Bob: Earl T., who got sober in Akron in 1938, who formed the Chicago nucleus of A.A., and whom Bill Wilson described as having been "soundly indoctrinated by Dr. Bob and the Akronites." But the purported description written in the Big Book is said to have been written by Early and to describe Dr. Bob's "six steps." Yet we have pointed out that there was no evidence of any steps used by Bob, and he said so; and the steps do not resemble Bill Wilson's two versions of the supposed six steps. They do contain language that Bob did not use and that Bill did use. Whether Earl T. actually wrote this belated story is a question that, of itself, deserves further investigation and analysis. Moreover, the language attributed to Dr. Bob is not language or even a subject that ever seems to have been entertained by Dr. Bob. In any event, Earl's story says there were six steps as follows:

1. Complete deflation [language that is more Wilsonian than Akron in character].

2. Dependence and guidance from a Higher Power ["Higher Power" is not a word used by Dr. Bob., who used Biblical language calling God "God" and "Heavenly Father."].

3. Moral inventory.

4. Confession.

5. Restitution.

6. Continued to work with alcoholics.[4] [omits God, Bible, message, and principles]

The language contained in the first item of the purported six steps just isn't what I have heard or read about Dr. Bob's characterizations of the alcoholic's problem. Bob typically spoke of your being licked, your being unable to quit, your need to be abstinent, and your need to avoid the first drink "that got you." The "higher power" stuff is not to be found, at least by me, in any language used by Bob, Anne Smith, Henrietta, or the Williamses—who were Earl T.'s real mentors and teachers. Moreover, Earl's story continues with mention of other Oxford Group practices, in addition to the supposed six that are numbered and attributed to Bob. The portion of the Earl T. story that lists an alleged six steps of Dr. Bob's

---

[4]Big Book, p. 292; See also *AA Comes of Age*, pp. 22-23.

looks to me like a complete fabrication—one that suited Bill's assertion that there were six word-of-mouth steps—and furthered his attempt to cloak his "six steps" with a post mortem insertion that provided a supposed origin with, and stamp of approval by, Dr. Bob stamp of approval But the Wilson stamp seems exemplified by the distinctly and exclusively Wilsonian language like "deflation" and "higher power."

One might even wonder if it matters in the grand scheme of things. Dr. Bob relied on the Bible. Bill mentioned six widely varying steps. Bill then fashioned 12 Steps attributable and attributed by him primarily to Sam Shoemaker. And Clarence Snyder launched the rapidly growing Cleveland program that embraced the Big Book, the Twelve Steps, the Four Absolutes, and the Bible. None of the roots has survived in today's mainstream A.A. And we have therefore focused on what can be learned and used from the Twelve and the sources that influenced the actual language Bill used in his Big Book and Twelve Steps.

Part 7:

Now let's consider the Steps in company with the three Bible parts Dr. Bob called "absolutely essential" lest some highly important spiritual resources of the A.A. program be forgotten

Bill Wilson and Dr. Bob both stated many times that the Sermon on the Mount contained the underlying philosophy of Alcoholics Anonymous. Bill also said the Book of James was such a favorite of the pioneers that many suggested calling their society "The James Club." As to Corinthians as a basic, Dr. Bob widely circulated the little book by Henry Drummond, titled *The Greatest Thing in the World* - a study of 1 Corinthians 13 - the so-called "love" chapter in the Bible. Moreover, Dr. Bob many times said that the old timers considered all three parts of the Bible–Matthew Chapters Five to Seven (called the "sermon on the mount"), the Book of James, and 1 Corinthians 13–to be "absolutely essential" to success in the program that Akron was developing.

For a recent, careful specific update of what I believe to be the James-Sermon-Corinthians ideas, themselves, see my latest title, *The James Club: The Original A.A. Program's Absolute Essentials* (http://www.dickb.com/JamesClub.shtml). This title studies in depth what I specifically describe as the non-step Akron Genesis of Alcoholics Anonymous.

No useful purpose would be served by actually quoting the three Bible parts in this Step guide. Nor even by quoting my own numerous detailed studies of them in my *James* title. Instead, you yourself would profit immensely by a study of each of these segments (one by one) in a Bible of your choice. When you have finished reading the particular Bible part, turn to any of the several Dick B. books which review, verse by verse, each Bible part and call attention to the Big Book or Step idea that was influenced by the segment. Particularly, see my *The James Club* work.

39

Better by far that you establish and conduct your own study as a Big Book/Bible Study Group. I have just finished writing a guide to show how such meetings can be conducted effectively, and I have previously published at least two studies of the parts themselves as they relate to A.A.. (See particularly, Appendix Two of Dick B. *Why Early A.A. Succeeded* Kihei, HI: Paradise Research Publications, Inc.; and *When Early AAs Were Cured and Why (Paradise Research Publications, Inc., supra)*. These analytical reference titles contain a detailed study of each of the Bible segments, and concurrently show where and how that particular segment, and the verses in it, impacted upon A.A. thinking and upon the development of the early "spiritual" program of recovery.

Here I propose a way that you can use to get well-grounded in the Bible segments without being side-tracked with meeting jabber or confusion with the Big Book and Clarence Snyder approaches.

First, Read the Remarks of the Founders about the Bible's Role in Early A.A.

See pages 225 to 228 of Dick B., *Why Early A.A. Succeeded, supra.* Better still, read Dick B., *The James Club*—all of it.

Then, Turn to the Book of James

Read this Book of James with great care. Its language is clear. Its messages are practical. It was much favored by the AA pioneers. Many words and phrases in the Big Book are easily identified as coming from James. You will also probably see some major basic ideas that AAs borrowed: ideas about patience, asking God's guidance, avoiding temptation, doing God's will, bearing no grudges, avoiding lying and envy, taking your own inventory, praying for others, and confessing your faults, one to another. Also as to the effectiveness of prayer by a righteous person.

A Study Plan

For The Book of James: When you have read the five chapters of James, follow up immediately by also reading my explanatory and detailed remarks about James, A.A., and the Big Book in *Why Early A.A. Succeeded, supra*, pp. 244-260 and *The James Club*. The James/A.A.

material is also discussed at length, verse by verse in my title, *When Early AAs Were Cured and Why*. Kihei, HI: Paradise Research Publications, Inc., 2003. You can then supplement your study by reviewing the comments in a devotional such as *The Runner's Bible*, which discusses many verses in James and was widely read by pioneer AAs.

Then, Tackle and Study the Sermon on the Mount

Read Chapters Four, Five, and Six of the Gospel of Matthew in your favorite Bible - preferably the *King James Version* if you wish to read the version A.A.'s Pioneers read and used. These three chapters in Matthew contain the entirety of the sermon that Jesus gave on the mount.

Follow this by reading my explanatory and detailed remarks in my titles *Why Early A.A. Succeeded, supra*, pp. 229 – 244; *When Early AAs Were Cured and Why, supra;* and all of *The James Club*, particularly the Sermon portions. .

Top that off by studying one of the topical commentaries on the "Sermon" Five were frequently read by pioneer AAs—titles by Oswald Chambers, Glenn Clark, Harry Emerson Fosdick, Emmet Fox, and E. Stanley Jones.

Bob and Anne read them all. See Dick B., *The Books Early AAs Read for Spiritual Growth*, 7th ed Kihei, HI: Paradise Research Publications, Inc., 1998; *Dr. Bob and His Library*, 3rd ed. Kihei, HI: Paradise Research Publications, Inc., 1998; and *Anne Smith's Journal*, 3rd ed., *supra*.

Conclude with a Study of 1 Corinthians 13

Read this short Bible chapter. Be sure you are reading in 1 Corinthians, and not 2 Corinthians.

Don't be baffled by the difficult "King's English." You can obtain a modern Bible like the *New International Version* or *New Jerusalem Bible* as well, and check out the words in those versions.

Then read my commentary in *Why Early A.A. Succeeded*, pp. 260-265, *When Early AAs Were Cured and Why,* and *The James Club*. These will make the Bible's words, their intent, and their relationship to the Big Book quite clear. In fact, I have laid out in comparative columns the Bible's words, the translated versions of others, and the pertinent Big Book language, seemingly borrowed from Corinthians.

Close out your study with Henry Drummond's all-time best-seller *The Greatest Thing in the World.* Early AAs loved it. It's a tiny book. Most pioneers read it. And Dr. Bob put great store in its importance for one who needs to change his life, be delivered from the curse of alcoholism, and walk in a way that God's Word spells out as loving conduct.

Note the Akron Difference

The first meeting, the first ideas, the first spiritual recovery program, and the first A.A. group all began in Akron, Ohio. The program was Bible based. Its principles and practices came primarily from those of the United Christian Endeavor Society of Dr. Bob's youth in St. Johnsbury, Vermont. They featured love and service. To that root, Akron added a unique focus on helping drunks. Akron emphasized the virtual necessity for hospitalizing drunks at the beginning. It also utilized Oxford Group ideas such as surrender, inventory, confession, and restitution. Its success rates and cures rested on one solid foundation—receiving and relying upon the power of the Holy Spirit that accompanied the acceptance of Jesus Christ as Lord and Saviour.

Part 8:

Studying the Steps
Mindful of Other Major Contributing
Literature

Early AAs Were Readers!

Early AAs were readers. Dr. Bob's Home was loaded with spiritual literature, and he read for at least an hour each and every night. He prized and circulated among AAs the books he read. He recommended many books to early AAs and their families, and he actually kept a logbook showing those to whom the books had been loaned and who were to return them. Anne Smith mentioned them in her journal. Henrietta Seiberling read and circulated them. Almost every Oxford Group title I have read, as well as the back covers of Sam Shoemaker's parish journal, provided the names and authors of recommended books. I've found them in the homes of Dr. Bob's kids, Henrietta Seiberling's kids, T. Henry Williams' daughter, Clarence Snyder's family, Dr. Bob's Home, Stepping Stones, the homes of Oxford Group activists, and in the personal libraries of Sam Shoemaker, his daughters, and religious associates. I've also found them in the hands of many AAs today.

Don't ignore this background material! There are those who erroneously try to suppress it in A.A. by claiming that such books and articles will confuse newcomers, that they will mislead AAs as to A.A. principles and practices, that AAs should only read "Conference Approved" literature, that other literature violates the Traditions,—in far too many situations— that they should be "banned" from A.A. meetings, and that reading such literature will get many AAs drunk. These absurd censorship maneuvers have even been applied to the Holy Bible—the source from which A.A.'s basic ideas came. Moreover, in increasingly stringent written opinions, the censorship efforts have proliferated. I have copies of letters on A.A. letterheads in which some local yokel has: (1) banned or endeavored to ban the reading of the Bible, the reading of Emmet Fox, and other supposedly "heretical" matter; (2) Removed or tried to remove such meetings from official meeting lists, and even (3) Successfully eliminated the meetings themselves. The intimidation is furthered by sending "copies" of such purported authoritative letters to various people at World Service and at Grapevine offices in New York—implying that the "big guns" of A.A. leadership, our supposed "big brothers," will get you if you don't look out. And it works. I know of several groups that just stopped using outside literature in meetings because of threats from know-it-all local AAs. Some too who have just left A.A. and gone elsewhere for learning and support.

Bill Wilson many times said that A.A. was a spiritual kindergarten. Early issues of the A.A. *Grapevine* frequently recommended outside literature. So did some of the publications by area central offices and intergroups headquarters. Both Bill Wilson and Anne Smith recommended outside reading. Both suggested consulting clergy for suggestions as to appropriate religious books to study. Dr. Bob actually circulated many such books among AAs and their families; and A.A. literature confirms this. Moreover, the tables at early meetings contained displays of literature for examination and swapping.

Akron AAs, and the Oxford Group itself, had a purpose in circulating Christian literature. The books were owned, loaned, used, and read for a reason: They were deemed to be helpful in expanding understanding and aiding healing. And the Bible/Oxford Group/Shoemaker books that were read by AAs numbered in the hundreds. Some were used in connection with topics discussed at meetings.

Several of my titles contain detailed bibliographies of all references mentioned herein. The most useful are *The Books Early AAs Read for Spiritual Growth, 7th ed.; Dr. Bob and His Library, 3rd ed.; Anne Smith's Journal, 1933-1939 3rd ed; The Good Book and The Big Book, 2d ed,; That Amazing Grace; Turning Point: A History of Early A.A.'s Spiritual Roots and Successes; New Light on Alcoholism, 2d ed.;* and *Making Known the Biblical Roots of Early A.A.* (http://www.dickb.com/titles.shtml).

Specific, Important Christian Literature That Impacted on A.A. Pioneers

- Rev. Sam Shoemakers's books and articles, particularly *Realizing Religion, Religion That Works, Children of the Second Birth, The Gospel According to You,* The *Conversion of the Church, Confident Faith,* and *Twice-Born Ministers.*

- Robert Speer's *The Principles of Jesus* and Henry Wright's *The Will of God and a Man's Lifework*, which contain the two actual sources of A.A.'s Four Absolutes.

- H.A. Walter's *Soul Surgery*, which is the source of, and explains, The Five C's that are the heart of the life-changing program A.A. codified from the Oxford Group.

- Professor Philip Marshall Brown's *The Venture of Belief* - a reliable source for understanding the A.A. ideas of "willingness," "came to believe," and "decision."

- B. H. Streeter's *The God Who Speaks* in which this great Bible scholar explains the many Biblical examples of God's "guidance" and ways of communicating with man.

- Rev. Harry Almond's *Foundations for Faith* - which, in later years, spelled out the Oxford Group life-changing art by explaining its catchy principles: "Sin is the problem; Jesus Christ is the cure; the result is a Miracle." Almond carefully cites the underlying Bible verses that gave rise to the principles.

- The many other authors and books I have discussed in Dr. Bob and His Library, 3rd ed. These deal with matters AAs were frequently taught: (a) Books on healing. (b) Books on prayer. (c) Bible devotionals. (d) Books on Jesus Christ. (e) Books on studying the Bible. (f) Books on Christianity and the mind. (g) Books on religious experiences.

New Thought Traces

You will find the roots of our ever-more-common A.A. mysticism in some of Wilson's A.A. language. Whatever the reason, Wilson appropriated New Thought and even ideas that we now call "New Age" from some he chose to call A.A. founders. Thus the long-dead Professor William James appears to have bequeathed almost directly to Bill such esoteric phrases as "higher power," "self-surrender," "turning point," and "varieties of religious experience." Even as to James, it must be acknowledged that Bill's friend Rev. Sam Shoemaker was a major, actual spokesman for the deceased Harvard professor. And William James, influenced as he was by the ideas of Emanuel Swedenborg, can be credited with much New Thought and New Age language that found its way into Wilson's writings.

Furthermore, Wilson's confusing novel talk of "fourth dimension," "Universal Mind," the "Great Reality," the "Spirit of the Universe," "higher power," and "cosmic consciousness" no doubt found its way into A.A. through New Thought writers such as Emmet Fox, Judge Thomas Troward, and James Allen whose works were read or heard by some. And there are many other authors such as Ralph Waldo Trine, Mary Baker Eddy, and the Fillmores whose ideas and phrases poured into A.A. from that same wellspring.

Still Other Contributors

You can get a full view and better understanding of the outside A.A. Step sources to which Bill ascribed various A.A. thinking. In fact, discussion of these sources was sometimes even omitted from mention by Wilson. Thus there is work to be done on what Dr. Carl Jung really thought and said to the Oxford Group's Rowland Hazard about "conversion." Look also beyond the Big Book's "Doctor's Opinion" and discover what Dr. William D. Silkworth really thought about "moral psychology" and about Jesus Christ as the "Great Physician" who could cure alcoholism. Learn too what the lay therapist Richard Peabody seems to have inflicted on Bill's language despite Peabody's failure in therapy, death as a drunkard, and untested, unproved statements that "there is no cure for alcoholism." The irony in Bill's borrowed Peabody phrases is that Peabody himself died of alcoholism it and thereby proved the inability of his own secular approaches to "cure" alcoholism, at least as his theories applied to his own life, methods, drinking habits, and ultimate demise.

Conclusions about the Variety of Unmentioned or Speculative Contributions

Don't guess, verify.

Don't pass on myths and fiction. Determine the source and validity of an account before embracing its ideas, or calling them "history."

Do have an honest, willing, and searching approach to learning the present-day facts about alcoholism, about A.A. itself, and about today's secularism and rejection of God within A.A.'s ranks and in

today's society. Jesus-bashing has wormed its way into the fabric of recovery news articles, "scholarly" studies, talk shows, and meetings. Until recent years there had been so little written about early A.A.'s real "spiritual" ideas and "religious" sources that mounds of fictitious legends had arisen about A.A.'s nature, roots, program, effectiveness, and source of power. Self-fabricated "not-god-ness," "spirituality," and other thinking akin to New Age words and lingo have crept almost unchallenged into recovery. language and literature. We certainly hear far more about treatment and meetings than we do about the Almighty. Fed by grants, treatment enthusiasm, anti-religious bias, and academic interests, the color of the Steps has been changed from a dim Christian white to a glaring, idolatrous, graying black—"powerlessness," "choosing your own conception of a god," "acceptance," "spiritual awakenings of an educational rather than spiritual variety," and "change"—but not religious or conversion in character .

Zealous unbelievers have sold part of today's A.A. fellowship itself on the speculative assertion that the Oxford Group was headed by an alleged Nazi, and amounted to little more than an heretical cult. In fact there seems to be more concern about cults than about churches and clergy. Some have asserted that the Bible disappeared from the A.A. scene "because it didn't work" and that reading the Bible instead of the Big Book would get AAs drunk. Some allege that most newcomers will run for cover and will retreat from the rooms the very moment they hear the word "God." Wilson even coined the derogatory phrase: "fear of being God-bitten." Some assert that an undefined and incomprehensible New Age "spirituality" stands as A.A.'s bulwark against ego-inflation, religion, and a supposed religious poisoning of today's pure, undefined, and irreligious mainstream. Some contend that the long-dead, failed, godless Washingtonian Movement provides A.A. with a model of how it could disintegrate if it were to tip-toe into outside issues—meaning the "God thing.". This nonsense ignores the central shortcoming of the Washingtonian movement—that it lacked reliance on God. Some have injected concepts that were never a part of early A.A. yet supposedly tell what the real A.A. program involves. These strange concepts have included higher powers, lack of cure, spiritual awakenings, and self-constructed prayers to a self-made god.

These ever-proliferating and diverse "recovery" philosophies have meant that one is hard-pressed to avoid the nonsense and learn the truth. I believed and still do believe that historical research and factual reporting can and will provide a good foundation for those who don't want to be "guessers" and do aspire to be accurate "spokes people"--even proponents of the original A.A. program of cures and high success rates. See Dick B. *Cured: Proven Help for Alcoholics and Addicts*. Kihei, HI: Paradise Research Publications, Inc., 2003.

Part 9:

Start Taking Your Steps Precisely As Directed by the Big Book—then make your judgments

Confusion Begins When Members Fashion Their Own Instructions

In my almost two decades of being actively and intimately involved in the A.A. fellowship, nothing has impressed and blessed me more, in approaching the Big Book and the Twelve Steps, than the seminars, tapes, and literature put out by Joe Mc Q. and Charlie P. of Arkansas. Since these two first began their Big Book Seminars, many others have put out literature and put on seminars to help people understand and activate A.A.'s real program of recovery as it can be found described in any of the ever-increasing number of editions of our basic text, *Alcoholics Anonymous.*

Nonetheless, it's surprising that you still find a host of perfectly sincere A.A. speakers making up wild interpretations of the meaning of Steps: "Powerlessness" over "people places and things" per the First Step. Your higher power can be a tree or a light bulb, using the Second Step "power-greater-than-ourselves" idea as their launching pad. Still others amuse and instruct you as to the Third Step by telling you the story of the three frogs on a log as illustrative of the priorities in Bill's language about deciding to get a new Director. Many immobilize progress in taking the Fourth Step by terror, fostering a sense of complete inability to write it out, and yet failing to tell sponsees where to find, how to follow, and what to do with the specific instructions of the Big Book. Many are encouraged to go to priests and therapists rather than risk telling their Fifth Step secrets to a big-mouthed sponsor. Then come the utterly baffling two paragraphs of the Big Book that are said to cover Bill's johnnie-come-lately Sixth and Seventh Steps and "separate the men from the boys." Just two paragraphs, with few knowing where they came from or how to explain them.. People often ridicule the importance of the Eighth Step, labeling it a step that "costs you nothing." When it comes to the Ninth Step, there are those who suggest writing letters to dead people you have wronged or setting up a "newcomer account" to do penance. Many just skip the Tenth Step or confuse it with the Eleventh Step despite the fact that the Tenth Step marks the real beginning of daily practice of step principles. Others have presumed to lead "classes" in how to listen to God—discarding the Biblically oriented Morning Watch, Quiet Hour, and Quiet Time concepts that were so important to the pioneers and their progenitors. Finally, there is the common tragedy in talking about the Twelfth Step and yet absolutely missing the boat on what constitutes a spiritual awakening, what is the "message" to be carried, and what "principles" are referred to in the Step.

This part of the Twelve Step Guide will not cover all the simple instructions as to "how to" in the Big Book. Actually, if it is carefully studied, the Big Book does a fair job of telling people how to "take" Steps Three through Eleven. It wanders excessively on the First Step and therein embeds the "disease concept" in concrete. It manufactures new religion in the Second Step. And it completely omits defining a spiritual awakening, the message, and the principles alluded to in the Twelfth Step words.

So, if you are going to avoid confusing private interpretations and avoid manufacturing your own method of taking the "steps," you should start with the basic ideas that Wilson actually placed in the Big Book where he sought to give "clear cut directions" on how to take his steps.

The instructions in the Big Book and the Step elements

Step One - Defines alcoholics as those who have lost the ability to control their drinking; who cannot stop drinking when they want to; or who drink too much once they begin. They are said to have an allergy of the body, an obsession of the mind, and a progressively worsening disease. Also that they have a "spiritual malady" founded on self-centeredness. The Big Book teaches that neither self-knowledge, will-power, fear, nor any human power can relieve a real alcoholic of his alcoholism. Like it or not, that's what you need to learn.

Step Two - Fashions a "self-made" religion (better described as a Wilson-made plan for atheists and agnostics), which has led to goofy gods for those who reject the Creator. It urges willingness as the key to faith, but does provide an excellent definition of sanity as recoiling from a hot flame. Much more simply, this Step should have stuck to the way it was before revisionists altered it. Previously, it simply called for belief in God and belief that He can restore the alcoholic to sane thinking. Nothing tough at all about that. Dr. Bob laid the choice out on a "take it or leave it" basis (See *DR. BOB and the Good Oldtimers*, p. 144). And, in my own experience with taking some 100 men through the steps, I've never had one say that he didn't believe in God and didn't believe that God could restore him to sane thinking. The long-standing, seasoned response to someone's alleged fear of being "God-bitten" has been: "If the word 'God' scares you out of these rooms, a bottle of booze will scare you back if you live that long." Crude, but effective!

Step Three - Emphasizes that the action part of the steps begins with a decision to entrust one's life to God's care. Argues for that decision by declaring that self-propulsion does not work in life, that this "self-willed" behavior can be labeled "ego-centricity," that replacing this "self-centeredness" involves two decisions–the decision to quit playing god and the decision to let God be God. It concludes with a "surrender" prayer which amounts to adopting "Thy will be done" as the surrender which assures obedience to God's ways. Revisionists soon added "as we understood Him" to assuage unbelievers. Bill led many to believe he didn't know where the phrase came from, and this caused the non-present Jim B. to claim—without ever having Bill confirm or deny—that he (Jim B.) had authored the phrase. But the phrase amounted to nothing more than an adoption of Sam Shoemaker's "act as if" ideas. If you eliminate the Shoemaker history, the phrase gives rise to manufactured nonsense gods, where it should merely have fostered an attempt to gain understanding of Yahweh the Creator, our God, by acting in obedience to His will. Shoemaker, Anne Smith, and many Oxford Group writers suggested that you "surrender as much of yourself as you know or understand to as much of God as you know or understand" And this is a far cry from developing your own, private interpretation of some New Age god.

Step Four - Unobtrusively adopts the Oxford Group definition of sin as anything that blocks us from God and others. It calls for a written moral inventory that identifies and requires the listing of four principal "sins" or "blocks" to God - resentment, fear, self-seeking and/or selfish sex, and harms to others. It also sets the stage for the Eighth Step list of harms. It is inconsistent in omitting from Step

Four instructions the listing of "dishonesty" as one of the sins to be inventoried in Step Four; while specifically mentioning this "defect" in the language of Steps Ten and Eleven. It does, however, call for rigorous honesty in following Fourth Step inventory instructions. Just honestly write down your resentments, fears, selfish acts, and harms to others. No big deal.

Step Five - Requires a long, thorough, and confidential "confession" of Step Four details to a close-mouthed, understanding friend (or cleric/therapist equivalent).

Step Six - Mixes up the Oxford Group/Biblical idea of *conviction* with the thought that one can somehow expect God to "remove" on demand *all* one's sins and shortcomings. Introduces "willingness" as a "loophole" both for the individual and a reserve excuse for any supposed failure on God's part. I don't hold that you've done much by "reading" the one-paragraph of instructions. I think you should decide what you've done wrong is wrong and requires God's forgiveness and help in changing direction.

Step Seven - Mixes up the Oxford Group/Biblical idea of conversion and the blotting out of sins past with an appeal to God to *remove* all the blocks, sins, and shortcomings. Includes another surrender prayer that is quite similar to that in the Third Step. I don't hold that you've done much by reading this paragraph either, or even by reciting its prayer. Early AAs accepted Christ, received forgiveness, prayed for help in having alcohol taken out of their lives, and ask God to help them live by Christian principles. Add it to the Big Book if you like.

Step Eight - Calls for making a list of "amends" that is drawn from the Fourth Step inventory, urges a "willingness to begin" restoration, and an appeal to God for help.

Step Nine – Gives detailed directions to be used in the process of making amends to those harmed; provides guides to the action, suggesting humility, honesty, fearlessness, and courtesy; and admonishes against harming others in the process. Without attribution, incorporates the Golden Rule, though not saying so. Good stuff except where Wilson does a cop-out on impurity.

Step Ten - Contains the best, most brief, and most coherent set of Step instructions in the Big Book - calling for continued action with the life-changing process and the daily application of the practices of the previous steps – confidentiality, inventory, confession, reformation, and restitution. Adds "love and tolerance" as the A.A. code and suggests working with others as part of the daily process. Simple, and I like it and keep it in mind daily.

Step Eleven - Considered in its best light, it calls for: An end-of-the-day review of how well the Steps have been practiced, particularly the Tenth Step, suggests a request for God's forgiveness where there has been failure; a plan to do better; and a "quiet time" in the morning. Makes a guarded reference to using devotionals, church, and religious literature; and adds a Biblical suggestion that anxiety, doubt, and anger be obviated through reliance on God throughout the day. Even quotes the Bible's "Thy will be done" as part of the solution.

I can't and don't re-invent the Eleventh Step. In fact, it corrupts some important Biblical ideas and removes others. But it does make me thankful that I study the Bible, pray, ask God for forgiveness and healing and guidance, and remember He's an ever-present help. Your church can tell you what's what. And the Big Book even suggests just that. It says: Make use   of what religious people have to offer. Then do so!

Step Twelve - Can be divided into three poorly phrased parts: (1) An awakening. (2) A message. (3) The living of "principles." The problem with this scanty presentation is that A.A. has never successfully defined its borrowed Oxford Group expressions "spiritual experience" and "spiritual awakening" though each was, in sequence, codified into the steps. Moreover, the wording misses the point it was intended to make – that access to, and utilization of, "Power" would be the result of taking the Steps. Having "universalized" some "god," and having eliminated the one, true, living Creator Yahweh, His Son Jesus Christ, the gift of the Holy Spirit; and the Bible, it leaves one bereft of the very transforming rebirth that the life-changing steps were intended to produce. So too, by focusing almost exclusively on practical ways to work with other drunks, the Big Book's Twelfth Step chapter moves to back-stage and out of sight the real message that Ebby gave so effectively to Bill–that God had done for Ebby what he could not do for himself. Finally, by eliminating the Bible and the Biblical essentials spelled out by Dr. Bob, the Big Book fails completely even to give a coherent, organized description of "the principles" that were to be "practiced." These principles are, or were, of course, those set forth in the Sermon on the Mount, the love verses of Corinthians, the practices espoused by the Book of James, and the commandments of God found throughout the Bible.

Stick to the Big Book Instructions

It would appear that every Twelve Step and/or "anonymous" and/or "self help" group has today developed its own basic text, wording of the Steps, and thoughts about a "higher powered" god. There are 12 Step Bibles. There are 12 Step work books. There are 12 Step prayer books. There are 12 Steps with and without God and with and without Jesus. There are "higher powered" steps. There are basic texts or pamphlets for virtually every type of anonymous, 12 Step group. And A.A. itself has spawned this diversity by its "singleness of purpose" dogma. Yet every Twelve Step Fellowship, therapist, treatment center, rehab, therapeutic community, and religious "recovery" group is almost certain to find itself in possession of "clients" suffering from a host of different "addictions"-- all of which are amenable to the healing power of Almighty God

What do you do with all this? Recovery programs, treatment philosophies, and research work are producing diminishing returns, coupled with increasing demands for a demonstrable solution. President George W. Bush perhaps put the solution best, saying there is no recovery without changing the heart. But that's a spiritual matter, and the President saw it that way in his own faith and miraculous cure. It's not something guaranteed by a mechanical march through steps.

Do you re-write the Twelve Steps? Do you write your own basic text, your own work book, or your own curriculum? If you do, will it specify its own special brand of a "higher power," "Steps," "meetings," "drunkalogs," "singleness of purpose," "spirituality," and mean that each entity has an incorporated service structure? The answer—but not the desideratum--seems to have been "yes." "Yes" to 200 or more separate "self help" or "anonymous" or "support" groups. Yes to a variety of "gods." Yes to story telling. Yes to varying and separate types of meetings. Yes to re-worded steps. And yes to a separate corporate entity with separate offices and service structure.

Many have seemed fearful of losing face, funds, facilitators, government approval, grants, or private insurance money if they didn't follow the decrepit, edited, non-A.A. models of past decades. Do you write a new recovery approach? One highly successful operator of therapeutic communities for prisoners told me he had "curricula" by the dozens. His actual approach is Christian. But each new recovery program seems to add new nonsense gods, new psychological gimmicks, and irreligious ideas. Do you stick a revised program embodied in a Bible–as several major Christian publishers did a decade ago? The answer should be that God doesn't need steps in His Word. He speaks to us of His will in His Word by revelation, not by Twelve Step ideas originally fashioned by a self-proclaimed former "conservative atheist" who belonged to no church, studied no Bible, accepted no organized religion, dumped Jesus Christ, and left the company of the originating crowd to which he belonged–"A First Century Christian Fellowship."

It may therefore sound strange to hear that I am an advocate of sticking to A.A. and to the Big Book when it comes to teaching and "taking" the 12 Steps. But many believe God had a hand in early A.A. So too the Constitution of the United States which has remained intact despite amendments, weird judicial interpretations, and corrupt officials who have administered it. Without these God-inspired foundations, there would be little to distinguish either Alcoholics Anonymous or the United States itself from autocratic, totalitarian, godlessly governed entities. Little to hold people together in the face of increasingly diverse ethnic, religious, racial, and political influxes.

Look at the A.A. foundations. Akron was the crucible. Wilson became the spokesman. A.A emerged as the product. Attention was focused on the suffering, their need for support, and the solution—"God could and would if He were sought. And that attention grew to unbelievable size. Better, we think, to work with these roots than to invent new, faltering, fumbling, all-purpose fellowships without success experiences. Better, we think, to foster interest in, and enthusiasm for, learning and understanding our history, founders, and roots as well as the end product currently developing.
.

The primary, successful structure is still present for all to see and use. If it can maintain its integrity, avoid disintegration, embrace love and tolerance, and live and let live both religious and non-religious viewpoints, perhaps it will serve as a rallying point for victory over alcohol and drugs, far more than proliferating, inexperienced, over-worked splinter experiments by religion, secularists, and scientists. The marvel of A.A. has far more been the cohesiveness of the fellowship than the effectiveness of its varied religious meanderings since Akron. There has been a core of long-term, freely administered understanding, sympathy, and support that has personally benefited me. And I am far from certain that those features would have been present in some shorter

55

term, profit motivated, dogmatically run, labor demanding, or inexperienced well-wishing splinter effort.

A.A.'s fellowship has lots to offer because of its very size, geographic spread, ready availability, and recognized name. Most of us know that the mere fellowship, as it presently exists, would not be enough to produce either cure or contentment. More AAs than are probably willing to admit it really know that Almighty God is at the heart of the program purpose.

And in fact the idea that not drinking and going to meetings will cure alcoholism and produce contentment hasn't proved itself. Whether right or wrong, productive or non-productive, religious or irreligious, the Twelve Steps have demanded and brought about a promised design for living, a promised behavioral change, and a promised abstinence to those who have given that solution their best. I see no reason why A.A. or analysis should try to confine the results by banning or criticizing other approaches to spiritual growth, Divine help, and miraculous cure. Let the nay-sayers say nay. But I can say it is still possible to study the Big Book; take the Twelve Steps; practice the "maintenance" steps; help others to a cure; enjoy the fellowship; be a Christian, a Bible student, and loyal servant of Almighty God and His son; and violate no "Traditions" of A.A. or any comparable Twelve Step group.

Such activities go on right now in the rooms of A.A. and can continue to do so. The starting point for newcomers is still the Big Book, not some private interpretation of spirituality and deity.

Part 10:

Consider This Possible Biblical View of the 12 Steps
Using History as Your Guide

Proposing for believers a view of the Twelve Steps in light of their historical, Biblical, and Big Book origins

We admitted we were licked; that alcohol, life-controlling excesses, and sins (if you prefer to call them that) had become our master; and that our lives had become unmanageable.

Romans 7:24-25: "O wretched man that I am! Who shall deliver me from the body of this death? I thank God through Jesus Christ our Lord. So then with the mind I myself serve the law of God; and with the flesh the law of sin." [These verses were quoted in part in one of the personal stories in the Big Book's First Edition].

We believed in God and that, if we first sought Him and His righteousness, He would give us sound minds, supply our needs, help us resist temptations, and deliver us from our troubles.

1 Corinthians 10:13: "There hath no temptation taken you but such as is common to man; but God is faithful, who will not suffer you to be tempted above that ye are able; but will with the temptation also make a way to escape, that ye may be able to bear it."

Hebrews 11:6—". . . for he that cometh to God must believe that he is. . .;"

Matthew 6:33—"But seek ye first the kingdom of God, and his righteousness, and all these things shall be added unto you."

2 Timothy 1:7—"For God hath not given us the spirit of fear, but of power, and of love, and of a sound mind. "

Philippians 4:19—   "But my God shall supply all your need according to his riches in glory by Christ Jesus."

Psalm 34:6—"This poor man cried, and the Lord heard him, and saved him out of all his troubles."

We decided to trust our Creator with all our heart, acknowledge Him in all our ways, and ask Him to direct all our paths, and become his children through a new birth.

Proverbs 3:5-6—"Trust in the Lord with all thine heart; and lean not unto thine own understanding. In all thy ways acknowledge him, and he shall direct thy paths."

We made a fearless, searching, and truthful inventory of such of our conduct as had been disobedient to God's will.

Matthew 7:1-5—"Judge not, that ye be not judged. For with what judgment ye judge, ye shall be judged; and with what measure ye mete, it shall be measured to you again. And why beholdest thou the mote that is in thy brother's eye, but considerest not the beam that is in thine own eye? Or how wilt thou say to thy brother, Let me pull out the mote out of thine eye; and behold, a beam is in thine own eye? Thou hypocrite, first cast out the beam out of thine own eye; and then shalt thou see clearly to cast out the mote out of thy brother's eye."

a. Made a list of God's standards for honesty, purity, unselfishness, and love - and specified where we had fallen short (Robert E. Speer, The Principles of Jesus. NY: Fleming H. Revell, 1902).

b. Listed God's commandments against resentment, self-seeking, dishonesty, fear, and harming others - and specifed where we had erred (Frank N. D. Buchman, Remaking the World. London: Blandford Press, 1961).

5.   We put these facts on the table, in full view, before God, another human being, and ourselves:

a.   Confessing our faults to God and asking His forgiveness.

1 John 1:9—"If we confess our sins, he is faithful to forgive us our sins, and to cleanse us from all unrighteousness."

b. Confessing our faults to another for prayer and healing

James 5:16—"Confess your faults one to another, and pray for one another, that ye may be healed. The effectual fervent prayer of a righteous man availeth much."

6. We became entirely ready to discard our disobedient ways and adopt God's ways.

Ecclesiastes 12:13—"Let us hear the conclusion of the whole matter. Fear God, and keep his commandments: for this is the whole duty of man."

7. We sought to walk by faith (having been born again of God's spirit) and be transformed by changing our thoughts, words, and deeds to conform to His will.

Romans 8:14—"For as many as are led by the Spirit of God, they are the sons of God."

Romans 15:1-2—"I beseech you therefore, brethren, by the mercies of God, that ye present your bodies a living sacrifice, holy, acceptable unto God, which is your reasonable service. And be not conformed to this world; but be ye transformed by the renewing of your mind, that ye may prove what is that good, and acceptable, and perfect, will of God."

8. We affirmed God's commands that we love Him and our neighbors and resolved to change our behavior accordingly and correct any harms done through our disobedience.

1 John 5:1-4—"Whosoever believeth that Jesus is the Christ is born of God: and every one that loveth him that begat loveth him also that is begotten of him. By this we know that we love the children of God, when we love God and keep his commandments. For this is the love of God, that we keep his commandments: and his commandments are not grievous. For whatsoever is born of God overcometh the world: and this is the victory that overcometh the world, even our faith."

9.   We made direct amends where our behavior had been contrary to God's will, restored for   wrongs   done,   and avoided harming others in the process.

Numbers 5:6-7—"Speak unto the children of Israel, When a man or woman shall commit any sin that men commit, to do a trespass against the Lord, and that person be guilty; Then they shall confess their sin which they have done: and he shall recompense his trespass with the principal thereof, and add unto it the fifth part thereof, and give it unto him against whom he hath trespassed."

10.   We continued taking these steps, watching and praying to guard against disobedience, excesses, and harms - and promptly changed when we were wrong

Matthew 26:41—"Watch and pray, that ye enter not into temptation: the spirit indeed is willing, but the flesh is weak."

We sought more knowledge of, and fellowship with, God through daily inventory, asking God's forgiveness when at fault, renewing our obedience to His will, and growing in our fellowship with Him through Bible study, prayer, and asking God's guidance.

John 5:39—"Search the scriptures; for in them ye think ye have eternal life: and they are they which testify of me."

12.   We acknowledged that our deliverance, forgiveness, spiritual power, and changes had come from the Creator. We

witnessed to what He had done for us; and we tried to glorify Him, in the name of His Son Jesus Christ, in thankfulness, love, and service.

1 Corinthians 15:57-58—"But thanks be to God, which giveth us the victory through our Lord Jesus Christ. Therefore, my beloved brethren, be ye stedfast, unmoveable, always abounding in the work of the Lord, forasmuch as ye know that your labour is not in vain in the Lord.")

Yeah, but….

Let's deal with the negatives before we close. To the foregoing views, there are many things that some AAs may say. The statements may, as a matter of courtesy, start with "Yeah, but." And the "yeah but" really means, "whatever you say, it's not for me."

There may be some understandable reasons for the hesitance or resistance. Maybe you use a different Bible than those who quote King James. Maybe you use one of the Twelve Step Bibles that list dozens of verses in connection with each Step. Maybe you have seen and believed one or more of the hundreds of lists that quote a step and then quote one or more Bible verses in connection with that step. Maybe you wonder if the pioneers used the foregoing verses at all. Maybe you question whether Bill Wilson took his steps from those verses. Maybe you think that all of this was rendered irrelevant when the chapter "We Agnostics" was written. Maybe you are a Jew, a Roman Catholic, a Muslim, a Buddhist, a Hindu, Hare Krishna, a humanist, an atheist, an agnostic, or embrace some other kind of religion or belief or unbelief at variance with the Scriptures above. Maybe you dislike the word "God." Maybe you dislike the words "Jesus Christ." Maybe you still are mad at the "Nuns." Maybe you call yourself a "recovering Catholic." Maybe you are not an Evangelical. Maybe you are not a Pentecostal. Maybe you are not a "mainline" Protestant. Maybe you are interested in Unity, Religious Science, Christian Science, Science of Mind, Theosophy, Swedenborg, Rudolph Steiner, New Thought, New Age, Tarot cards, crystals, beads, or "Eastern" religions. Maybe you are convinced that mentioning the word "God" will drive people out of meetings. Maybe you think the mention of Jesus Christ is violative of the Twelve Traditions. Maybe you think "inclusive" means everyone you agree with. Maybe you think "exclusive" means kicking out anyone you disagree with. Maybe you think they both mean that doors should be open to anyone, anywhere, of any race, color, creed, or political affiliation. Perhaps you are a hottentot.

There is probably one - maybe many more – of each of the above, wandering in and out and through A.A. meetings all over the United States, let alone in the million-man membership abroad.

How then can you expect such people to read about the early A.A. Christian Fellowship, its daily use of the Bible, its acceptance of Jesus Christ, its recommendations about church, its pre-occupation with Christian literature and Christian devotionals! Is all that stuff just history fluff or a downright irritant to our diverse and floating mass of people, many of whom are still sick, partly brain damaged, angry, afraid, reclusive, or emotionally unstable.

You can take the position of James Houck, today's A.A. member with the longest sobriety, and possibly the oldest person in A.A. Jim is still talking about the Bible, about the Oxford Group, and about God and His son Jesus Christ. Jim didn't come within miles of Akron A.A. for years and years and years. He just formulated his ideas based on his Methodist beliefs, his quitting alcohol cold turkey, his enthusiasm for the Oxford Group, his acquaintance with Rev. Sam Shoemaker, and his acquaintance with Bill Wilson—who attended Oxford Group meetings in Jim's home state of Maryland. Jim enjoys life, sobriety, and witnessing. Jim doesn't say, "Yeah but." In endorsing my "Cured" title, for example, Jim wrote: "Heartily endorsing Dick's new book and saying: If you take God out of the recovery picture, you have nothing." Jim has been sober since a date either immediately before or immediately after Bill Wilson got sober and months before A.A. was founded. Nobody's thrown him out of the two A.A. meetings I attended and when he spoke.

But how about the others – the two million members, most of whom may have little or no interest in church, religion, the Bible, or Christianity? Are we to cover our roots, ignore our history, and march to some ill-defined secular tune?

So what!

I can only say that neither Jim with his Oxford Group orientation, nor any of the other two million or so members bother me at all in this stage of my almost twenty years of sobriety. I don't think I would be sober if I hadn't joined A.A. I don't think I would have realized the seriousness of alcoholism if I hadn't quit booze, had seizures, and seen my resultant life in a state of total shambles. I was licked and really didn't know why. The closest door was that which opened into A.A.'s rooms. And I marched through. I quit the booze cruise. I dived into A.A. deeply. And I haven't left.

However, I am equally clear that my present sobriety wouldn't be worth a fig if I hadn't grasped where God fits in the picture, in my recovery, and in my life. The guilt, the shame, the disgrace, the sickness, the bewilderment, and the economic disasters could never have been faced, handled, and overcome by me without my firm reliance on my Creator, my continued study of the Bible, and my open willingness to witness the victory to others.

Let anyone say, "Yeah but." My reply is "So what." I want as many people as possible to know the virtually ignored and concealed, accurate early history of A.A. I want them to have as much of a chance as the Akron pioneers had when they sought cure by Divine Aid—as Bill called it. Our Pioneers were "medically incurable." They were in despair. And God helped them. They then subscribed to a basic text that made that point clear. We need to know **their beliefs, practices, message, records, and successes.**

There is room for all of us. And there is probably a desperate need for those of us who can shed light on and protest the "any god," "not-god," misunderstood "spirituality," and religion bashing in today's fellowship.

Now what about Jesus Christ?

Let's look at A.A. History again. The Oxford Group, from which A.A. sprang, was "A First Century Christian Fellowship." Its founder was a Lutheran Minister. Its "American leader"–to use Wilson's expression–was an Episcopal rector. In Akron and in New York the early "alcoholic squads" were an integral part of the Oxford Group for a time. Later, each split. For different reasons, and at different times. But Akron retained its Bible emphasis and belief in the Four Absolutes. New York focused on the Oxford Group program and practices. But it did so *sub silencio*. It was hardly forthright in admitting the fact. Clarence Snyder in Cleveland openly embraced the Big Book, the Steps, the Oxford origins, the Bible, and the Four Absolutes.

The Akron pioneers were largely Protestant, atheist, or agnostic, they said. Yet they turned to Jesus Christ as their Lord and Saviour and sought to become born again through belief in Christ. On their very heels, the next to arrive were hosts of Roman Catholics. And, whether they took comfort in the ministrations of Sister Ignatia in Akron or in the impact of Father Ed Dowling in New York, they certainly did not abandon their fealty to Jesus Christ. Next came a small contingent of those from the Jewish faith; and there seemed to be no ruckus from them about Christ–just dependence on Yahweh, the God of Jesus Christ, the Jews, and the Bible. Concurrently came many of little, other, or no faith.

And what did all these early birds ultimately do with Jesus and God? For sure, they didn't abandon them. They just began soft-pedaling that whole story. But there also seemed to be a unique concern about helping Buddhists, Swedenborgians, and hottentots. I'm not sure most AAs have ever met any. But some seemed worried sick that these people might be offended if Jesus Christ is ever again mentioned. Still, no effort was made to embrace, nor enthusiasm expressed for their beliefs or to add their precepts to the mix. The answer was best given by Bill Wilson to his Roman Catholic advisor and editor, Father John C. Ford, S.J.

Bill told Father Ford that he didn't really care what the Buddhists did with the Twelve Steps. In other words, implied Bill, A.A. was now open to all–atheists, agnostics, unbelievers, Christians, Muslims, Buddhists, and hottentots. Its modified version of the original Twelve Steps remained unchanged in language for many decades. Until recently, A.A. nonetheless increased in numbers and popularity all over the world. But it was left to the members to join, or not to join, their own religions, denominations, and sects. They certainly were not given any mandate or encouragement that caused them to condemn or require conformity to any particular religious or irreligious group.

So today, what about Jesus Christ? What about you! Suppose you want to follow the Way. If you do, I'd suggest you read the Bible, join a church, or become baptized with water or the Holy Spirit if you want to know more. You don't have to change A.A. or abandon the Twelve Steps to do that. As a matter of fact, you will learn far more about God, Jesus Christ, and the Bible outside of A.A. today than you will inside. A.A. has changed so much and diminished in religious fervor so much that it offers little encouragement to those who are zealous worshippers.

What should they do? My suggestion is really simple: Just get to know A.A. history. Get to know A.A.'s Big Book. Get to know A.A.'s Twelve

Steps and how to take them. Pick up on their principles that are consistent with your beliefs, just as you do in the Boy Scouts, the Rotary Club, the football team, the college fraternity, and the political party of your choice. You don't run the world, and you don't need to. Let go, and let God! That's what early AAs decided to do, whatever their religious preferences. I don't know of any mass expulsion of Hottentots, Jews, Hindus, or Presbyterians in early A.A.

Neither A.A. Christians, nor Jews, nor any other believers need a defense attorney. They don't need to launch reform movements. They don't need to leave A.A. They don't even need to bless others with their particular religious viewpoints. They certainly shouldn't bash anyone for talking about God, church, the Bible, Jesus Christ, Buddhism, atheism, or theosophy. There is no A.A. creed to which someone must subscribe. But there is a history they should know—especially if they are involved in contempt prior to investigation.

Recovery for believers comes through God, not by way of some misguided, loud-mouthed anti-religious bigot who feels compelled to try intimidating believing newcomers. You can vote with your feet and leave those characters with their resentments and megaphones in the meetings they try to dominate. You can and should seek out the person who still suffers. You can and should inform that person of your own cure, of your own religious convictions, and of his choices. You can and should make him aware of A.A.'s beginnings and cures and successes. You can and should tell him that he can be cured in or out of A.A., that he can hold and study whatever religious ideas he chooses, that out-spoken bigots do not represent or govern A.A.—however loud their voices may ring. You can and should make the new person aware of what God has done for you that you could not do for yourself. Give him the facts, the choice, and a decision.

That was the very first message—the one that Ebby Thacher carried to Bill Wilson and that stopped Bill in his tracks in his refusal to rely on religion. Ebby told Bill, "I've got religion." That was the message that caused Bill to go to the Calvary Rescue Mission and make his decision for Christ and write "For sure I was born again." Few know it, but manuscripts show that Bill himself then wrote, "I've got religion." That was the message by Ebby that prompted Bill to go to Towns Hospital, follow Ebby's suggestions, and soon stand on the conversion experience that left him free from alcoholism for good.

Believers can pull out their Bible, as I did in despair at the VA psych ward at eight months of sobriety. I read and memorized the following verse. I read it again and again until I believed it:

"Ye are of God, little children, and have overcome them: because greater is he that is in you, than he that is in the world" (1 John 4:4).

There is nothing at all that should prevent you from learning all about the Twelve Steps and their roots and then forthrightly telling your newcomer:

1. Obtain and read the Big Book. Then get someone to teach you from it.

2. Resolve to take, and take, the Twelve Steps with a sponsor who uses the instructions in the Big Book.

3. If you are a Christian or want to become a Christian in A.A., be sure to get a sponsor who knows where A.A. came from, who talks freely about God, Jesus Christ, and the Bible. One who has been delivered from the power of darkness .One who can and will show you how you too can overcome and be delivered just as he was. One who knows and studies   the Bible and can share freely with you as a believer. And one who knows the "solution" is the beginning and our Heavenly Father's will the end.

4. Fellowship with like-minded believers.

5. Don't look for the faults in A.A. Look for the virtues. And applaud them

End

About the Author

Dick B. writes books on the spiritual roots of Alcoholics Anonymous. They show how the basic and highly successful biblical ideas used by early AAs can be valuable tools for success in today's A.A. His research can also help the religious and recovery communities work more effectively with alcoholics, addicts, and others involved in Twelve Step programs.

The author is an active, recovered member of A.A.; a retired attorney; and a Bible student. He has sponsored more than one hundred men in their recovery from alcoholism. Consistent with A.A.'s traditions of anonymity, he uses the pseudonym "Dick B."

He has had twenty-eight titles published including: *Dr. Bob and His Library*; *Anne Smith's Journal, 1933-1939*; *The Oxford Group & Alcoholics Anonymous*; *The Akron Genesis of Alcoholics Anonymous*; *The Books Early AAs Read for Spiritual Growth*; *New Light on Alcoholism: God, Sam Shoemaker, and A.A.*; *Courage to Change* (with Bill Pittman); *Cured: Proven Help for Alcoholics and Addicts*; *The Good Book and The Big Book: A.A.'s Roots in the Bible*; *That Amazing Grace: The Role of Clarence and Grace S. in Alcoholics Anonymous*; *Good Morning!: Quiet Time, Morning Watch, Meditation, and Early A.A.*; *Turning Point: A History of Early A.A.'s Spiritual Roots and Successes, Hope!: The Story of Geraldine D., Alina Lodge & Recovery; Utilizing Early A.A.'s Spiritual Roots for Recovery Today; The Golden Text of A.A.; By the Power of God; God and Alcoholism; Making Known the Biblical History of A.A.; Why Early A.A. Succeeded*; *Comments of Dick B. at The First Nationwide A.A. History Conference*; *Henrietta Seiberling: Ohio's Lady with a Cause;* and *The James Club*. The books have been the subject of newspaper articles and reviews in *Library Journal, Bookstore Journal, The Living Church, Faith at Work, Sober Times, Episcopal Life, Recovery News, Ohioana Quarterly, The PHOENIX*, and *The Saint Louis University Theology Digest*. They are listed in the biographies of major addiction center, religion, and religious history sites. He has published over 150 articles on his subject, most posted on the internet.

Dick is the father of two sons (Ken and Don) and has two granddaughters. As a young man, he did a stint as a newspaper reporter. He attended the University of California, Berkeley, where he received his A.A. degree with Honorable Mention, majored in economics, and was elected to Phi Beta Kappa in his Junior year. In the United States Army, he was an Information-Education Specialist. He received his A.B. and J.D. degrees from Stanford University, and was Case Editor of the Stanford Law Review. Dick became interested in Bible study in his childhood Sunday School and was much inspired by his mother's almost daily study of Scripture. He joined, and was president of, a Community Church affiliated with the United Church of Christ. By 1972, he was studying the origins of the Bible and began traveling abroad in pursuit of that subject. In 1979, he became much involved in a Biblical research, teaching, and fellowship ministry. In his community life, he was president of a merchants' council, Chamber of Commerce, church retirement center, and homeowners' association. He served on a public district board and has held offices in a service club.

In 1986, he was felled by alcoholism, gave up his law practice, and began recovery as a member of the Fellowship of Alcoholics Anonymous. In 1990, his interest in A.A.'s Biblical/Christian roots was sparked by his attendance at A.A.'s International Convention in Seattle. He has traveled widely; researched at archives, and at public and seminary libraries; interviewed scholars, historians, clergy, A.A. "old-timers" and survivors; and participated in programs and conferences on A.A.'s roots.

The author is the owner of Good Book Publishing Company and has several works in progress. Much of his research and writing is done in collaboration with his older son, Ken, an ordained minister, who holds B.A., B.Th., and M.A. degrees. Ken has been a lecturer in New Testament Greek at a Bible college and a lecturer in Fundamentals of Oral Communication at San Francisco State University. Ken is a computer specialist and director of marketing and research in Hawaii ethanol projects.

Dick is a member of the American Historical Association, Research Society on Alcoholism, Alcohol and Drugs History Society, Organization of American Historians, The Association for Medical Education and Research in Substance Abuse, Coalition of Prison Evangelists, Christian Association for Psychological Studies, and International Substance Abuse and Addictions Coalition. He is available for conferences, panels, seminars, and interviews.

Good Book Publishing Company Order Form

(Use this form to order Dick B.'s titles on early A.A.'s roots and successes)

Qty.	Titles by Dick B.	Price	
_____	*A New Way In*	$19.95 ea.	$ _____
_____	*A New Way Out*	$19.95 ea.	$ _____
_____	*Anne Smith's Journal, 1933-1939*	$22.95 ea.	$ _____
_____	*By the Power of God: A Guide to Early A.A. Groups and Forming Similar Groups Today*	$23.95 ea.	$ _____
_____	*Cured! Proven Help for Alcoholics and Addicts*	$23.95 ea.	$ _____
_____	*Dr. Bob and His Library*	$22.95 ea.	$ _____
_____	*Dr. Bob of Alcoholics Anonymous*	$24.95 ea.	$ _____
_____	*God and Alcoholism*	$21.95 ea.	$ _____
_____	*Good Morning! Quiet Time, Morning Watch, Meditation, and Early A.A.*	$22.95 ea.	$ _____
_____	*Henrietta B. Seiberling*	$20.95 ea.	$ _____
_____	*Introduction to the Sources and Founding of A.A.*	$22.95 ea.	$ _____
_____	*Making Known the Biblical History and Roots of Alcoholics Anonymous*	$24.95 ea.	$ _____
_____	*New Light on Alcoholism: God, Sam Shoemaker, and A.A.*	$24.95 ea.	$ _____
_____	*Real Twelve Step Fellowship History*	$23.95 ea.	$ _____
_____	*That Amazing Grace: The Role of Clarence and Grace S. in Alcoholics Anonymous*	$22.95 ea.	$ _____
_____	*The Akron Genesis of Alcoholics Anonymous*	$23.95 ea.	$ _____
_____	*The Books Early AAs Read for Spiritual Growth*	$21.95 ea.	$ _____
_____	*The Conversion of Bill W.*	$23.95 ea.	$ _____
_____	*The First Nationwide A.A. History Conference*	$22.95 ea.	$ _____
_____	*The Golden Text of A.A.*	$20.95 ea.	$ _____
_____	*The Good Book and the Big Book: A.A.'s Roots in the Bible*	$23.95 ea.	$ _____
_____	*The Good Book-Big Book Guidebook*	$22.95 ea.	$ _____
_____	*The James Club and the Original A.A. Program's Absolute Essentials*	$23.95 ea.	$ _____
_____	*The Oxford Group and Alcoholics Anonymous*	$23.95 ea.	$ _____
_____	*Turning Point: A History of Early A.A.'s Spiritual Roots and Successes*	$29.95 ea.	$ _____
_____	*Twelve Steps for You*	$21.95 ea.	$ _____
_____	*Utilizing Early A.A.'s Spiritual Roots for Recovery Today*	$20.95 ea.	$ _____
_____	*When Early AAs Were Cured and Why*	$23.95 ea.	$ _____
_____	*Why Early A.A. Succeeded*	$23.95 ea.	$ _____

(Order Form continued on the next page)

Good Book Publishing Company Order Form

(continued from the previous page)

Order Subtotal: $ _____

Shipping and Handling (S&H) **: $ _____

(** For Shipping and Handling, please add 10% of the Order Subtotal for U.S. orders or 15% of the Order Subtotal for international orders. The minimum U.S. S&H is $5.60. The minimum S&H for Canada and Mexico is US$ 9.95. The minimum S&H for other countries is US$ 11.95.)

Order Total: $ _____

Credit card: VISA   MasterCard   American Express   Discover (circle one)

Account number: _____ Exp.: _____

Name: _____ (as it is on your credit card, if using one)

(Company: _____)

Address Line 1: _____

Address Line 2: _____

City: _____ State/Prov.: _____

Zip/Postal Code: _____ Country: _____

Signature: _____ Telephone: _____

Email: _____

No returns accepted. Please mail this Order Form, along with your check or money order (if sending one), to: Dick B., c/o Good Book Publishing Company, PO Box 837, Kihei, HI 96753-0837. Please make your check or money order (if sending one) payable to "Dick B." in U.S. dollars drawn on a U.S. bank. If you have any questions, please phone: 1-808-874-4876 or send an email message to: dickb@dickb.com. Dick B.'s web site: www.DickB.com.

If you would like to purchase Dick B.'s entire 29-volume reference set on early A.A.'s roots and successes (and how those successes may be replicated today) at a substantial discount, please send Dick B. an email message or give him a call.

Paradise Research Publications, Inc.
PO Box 837
Kihei, HI 96753-0837
(808) 874-4876
Email: dickb@dickb.com
URL: http://www.dickb.com/index.shtml
http://www.dickb-blog.com